Study Guide for Decoding Othello

With Typical Questions and Answers

Steven Smith

Sherwood Press

CONTENTS

How to use this guide — 1

1. Historical background to William Shakespeare's Othello — 2

2. Why do students read Othello — 4

3. Similarities with Othello and other Shakespeare's plays — 6

4. Understanding of literature and culture — 8

5. Describe the themes — 10

6. Character analysis — 12

7. Language and rhetoric — 14

8. Understanding tragedy — 17

9. Relevance to contemporary issues — 19

10. Race and otherness theme — 21

11. Gender and power — 23

12. Religion and culture — 25

13. Social hierarchy and military culture — 27

14. Manipulation and deception — 29

15. Jealousy theme — 31

16. Manipulation and desception theme — 33

17. Race and otherness theme — 35

18. Love and betrayal theme ... 37

19. Identity and reputation theme ... 39

20. Gender theme ... 41

21. Imagery and metaphor ... 43

22. Animal imagery ... 45

23. Irony ... 47

24. Soliloquy ... 49

25. Prose and verse ... 51

26. Othello's language ... 53

27. Tragic Hero ... 55

28. Race and otherness ... 57

29. Gender dynamics ... 59

30. Manipulation and 'Fake News' ... 62

31. Jealousy and toxic masculinity ... 64

32. Power and corruption ... 67

33. Summary of the play ... 69

34. Act 1 ... 72

35. Act 2 ... 74

36. Act 3 ... 76

37. Act 4 ... 78

38. Act 5 ... 80

39. Main characters ... 82

40. Describe Othello ... 84

41. Describe Iago — 86

42. Describe Desdemona — 88

43. Describe Cassio — 90

44. Describe Emilia — 92

45. Minor characters — 94

46. Important relationships — 96

47. Othello and Desdemona's relationship — 99

48. Othello and Iago's relationship — 101

49. Desdemona and Emilia s relationship — 103

50. Iago and Emilia's relationship — 105

51. Iago and Roderigo's relationship — 107

52. Conflicts — 109

53. What makes this play a tragedy — 115

54. Climax of the play — 117

55. Resolution of the play — 119

56. Moral of this play — 121

57. Famous lines from the play — 124

HOW TO USE THIS GUIDE

This analysis of William Shakespeare's "Othello" intends to offer a study guide to readers who need a more in-depth view of the story.

This book is divided into questions, so the answers appear in a short essay style and may include repeated information. The questions are typical of what a high school student may experience.

I think all important questions have been directly or indirectly answered. However, if you, the reader, feel something is missing, please reach out to me, and I will add it!

Happy studying!

Steven Smith

stevensmithvo@gmail.com

— · —

HISTORICAL BACKGROUND TO WILLIAM SHAKESPEARE'S OTHELLO

"Othello, the Moor of Venice" is a tragedy written by William Shakespeare around 1603. The play is set in Venice and Cyprus during the late 16th century, a time when Venice was one of the most powerful city-states in the world, known for its maritime strength, wealth, and significant influence in the Mediterranean region. It was also a time of tension between Christian Europe and the Ottoman Empire, which included Cyprus until it was occupied by Venice in 1571. These historical events and cultural circumstances form the backdrop to the play's events.

The play's main character, Othello, is a Moor. Moors were originally North African Muslims who conquered Spain in the 8th century but by Shakespeare's time, the term was more generally used to describe anyone of African or Middle Eastern descent. Despite its racial undertones, the play provides a complicated depiction of Othello, who rises to the high ranks of the Venetian military despite his foreign origins and the prevalent prejudices of the time.

The story of Othello itself is derived from a short narrative in "Gli Hecatommithi", a collection of tales published in 1565 by the Italian writer, Giovanni Battista Giraldi, also known as Cinthio. The tale, "Un Capitano Moro," provides the basic plot that Shakespeare developed into Othello.

During the Elizabethan era, when Shakespeare was writing, the public had a mixed perception of Moors and Africans. On one hand, they were seen as exotic and fascinating, while on the other hand, they were often viewed with suspicion and fear. "Othello" plays on these perceptions and presents themes of jealousy, racism, betrayal, and revenge, all framed within the military and political tensions of its historical setting.

Shakespeare used the cultural and social dynamics of his time, such as gender norms and racial attitudes, to add depth to his characters and their motivations. For instance, Desdemona's rebellion against her father Brabantio to marry Othello goes against the expectations of a patriarchal society, and the character of Iago capitalizes on the racial and cultural anxieties of the period to manipulate those around him. Furthermore, the tension between Venice, representing the Christian West, and the Ottoman Turks, representing the Islamic East, serves as a backdrop to the personal conflict within Othello, who straddles these two worlds.

While "Othello" reflects certain historical realities of its time, it is not a historical play per se, but a drama that uses its historical setting to explore timeless human issues and emotional experiences.

— · —

WHY DO STUDENTS READ OTHELLO

There are several reasons why students read "Othello," not only for its historical significance as a work of one of the greatest playwrights in history, but also for its deep exploration of human nature and its relevance to contemporary issues. Here are a few specific reasons:

1. **Understanding Literature and Culture:** "Othello" is one of Shakespeare's most famous plays and an essential piece of English literature. Understanding Shakespeare's works is crucial to understanding the evolution of English literature and Western culture more broadly.

2. **Exploration of Themes:** The play explores various universal themes such as jealousy, racism, love, betrayal, revenge, and manipulation, which are as relevant today as they were in Shakespeare's time. Analyzing these themes can lead to rich discussions and critical thinking.

3. **Character Analysis:** The characters in "Othello" are complex and multifaceted, providing ample opportunities for students to engage in character analysis. For example, Iago is often considered one of literature's most sinister villains, and his manipulative tactics provide a lot of material for psychological analysis.

4. **Language and Rhetoric:** Shakespeare's use of language is another reason students read his works. "Othello" showcases Shake-

speare's ability to use and manipulate language, with many examples of metaphor, simile, personification, and other rhetorical devices. It provides an opportunity to study these techniques in depth.

5. **Understanding of Tragedy:** "Othello" is a classic example of a tragedy. Reading and understanding this play can provide insights into the characteristics and structure of tragic drama, which is a staple of literature.

6. **Relevance to Contemporary Issues:** Despite being written over 400 years ago, "Othello" remains relevant to contemporary issues. It deals with race, otherness, and prejudice, themes that resonate with present-day social issues. As such, the play can be a springboard for discussions about race, identity, and social dynamics in the modern world.

7. **Interdisciplinary Study:** "Othello" provides opportunities for interdisciplinary study. It can be analyzed from different perspectives, including historical, sociological, psychological, and philosophical viewpoints.

Overall, reading "Othello" offers students a comprehensive learning experience that involves critical thinking, comprehension, and analysis skills while engaging with important themes and issues.

— · —

SIMILARITIES WITH OTHELLO AND OTHER SHAKESPEARE'S PLAYS

There are indeed similarities between "Othello" and other plays by Shakespeare, such as "Macbeth," "Hamlet," and "Romeo and Juliet," mainly in the themes, character types, and dramatic devices used.

1. Tragic Heroes and Fatal Flaws: Much like "Macbeth" and "Hamlet," "Othello" also features a tragic hero who is brought down by his fatal flaw, or 'hamartia.' Othello, like Macbeth and Hamlet, is a fundamentally good man who is led to his downfall by a combination of external manipulations and his own insecurities. For Othello, this fatal flaw is his extreme jealousy; for Macbeth, it's unchecked ambition; and for Hamlet, it's indecision.

2. Manipulation and Deceit: Another common thread is the theme of manipulation and deceit. Just as Iago tricks Othello into believing that Desdemona is unfaithful, Lady Macbeth manipulates Macbeth into murdering King Duncan in "Macbeth," and Claudius deceives the entire kingdom about the true nature of King Hamlet's death in "Hamlet."

3. Love and Misunderstandings: "Othello" also shares with "Romeo and Juliet" a focus on the theme of love and the tragic consequences of misunderstandings and societal prejudices. Both plays explore the dangers of intense passion—be it love or jeal-

ousy—and feature a tragic ending because of miscommunications.

4. Power and Social Hierarchy: Much like "King Lear" or "Macbeth," "Othello" explores the dynamics of power and social hierarchy. In all these plays, the struggle for power leads to chaos, disorder, and tragedy.

5. Use of Soliloquy: In terms of dramatic techniques, Shakespeare's use of soliloquy is a common feature across his plays. In "Othello," Iago's soliloquies reveal his manipulative plans to the audience, much like Hamlet's famous "To be or not to be" soliloquy in "Hamlet" gives insight into his inner turmoil.

6. Symbolism and Imagery: Shakespeare's use of symbolism and imagery is another common feature. The green-eyed monster of jealousy in "Othello," the blood imagery in "Macbeth," and the ghost in "Hamlet" are all examples of symbolic elements used to enhance themes and character development.

Therefore, while "Othello" is unique in its narrative and characterisation, it shares common themes, character archetypes, and dramatic techniques with other Shakespearean plays, illustrating the consistency of Shakespeare's exploration of human nature and his masterful use of dramatic devices.

UNDERSTANDING OF LITERATURE AND CULTURE

Understanding literature and culture through "Othello" involves seeing the play not only as a story about individuals but also as a reflection of the society and time in which it was created. "Othello" provides insights into Elizabethan and Jacobean England's views on race, power, gender, and the clash of cultures, which are all woven into the plot and themes of the play.

1. **Race and Otherness**: Othello is described as a "Moor," which in Shakespeare's time was used to refer to individuals of North African, Middle Eastern, or even South Asian descent. His racial difference is a central element of the play and is used by other characters to marginalize and discredit him. For example, Iago often dehumanizes Othello with animalistic metaphors ("old black ram"), exploiting existing prejudices to further his own schemes. This portrayal gives us insights into the Elizabethan view of race and the outsider.

2. **Gender and Power**: The play reflects the patriarchal society of its time, where women were seen as subordinate to men. Desdemona's decision to marry Othello against her father's wishes and her assertive defense of her choice ("I do perceive here a divided duty") was a bold move. However, despite her initial assertiveness, Desdemona falls victim to the expectations of female obedience and passivity, which ultimately leads to her tragic end.

3. **Religion and Culture**: The setting of the play is amidst the tension between Christian Venice and the Islamic Ottoman Empire. The Venetian society, represented by characters like Brabantio and Roderigo, often views Othello through the lens of his religious and cultural difference, which contributes to the sense of him as an outsider, despite his military achievements.

4. **Social Hierarchy and Military Culture**: Othello's high rank in the Venetian military, despite being a foreigner, shows the importance of military prowess in Elizabethan society. However, the tension between Othello's public status and private downfall reflects the complex relationship between personal life and public duties in this society.

5. **Manipulation and Deception**: Iago's manipulation and deceit are tools that reveal the dangers of rhetoric and false appearances in a society that values reputation and public image. His ability to "wear my [his] heart upon my [his] sleeve" illustrates the cynical view of interpersonal relationships and the destructiveness of deceit, which may reflect broader social anxieties in Shakespeare's time.

Thus, through "Othello", we gain a complex understanding of the socio-cultural dynamics of Elizabethan and Jacobean England. The play highlights the period's concerns, anxieties, and values, providing a window into how these societies perceived issues such as race, power, gender, and the clash of cultures.

— · —

DESCRIBE THE THEMES

"Othello" is a complex tragedy that explores many themes. Here are some of the most prominent:

1. **Jealousy**: This is one of the central themes in "Othello". It is most evident in Othello's transformation from a rational and loving husband to a murderous one, driven by unfounded jealousy. This is manipulated by Iago, who warns Othello, "O, beware, my lord, of jealousy; It is the green-eyed monster which doth mock the meat it feeds on." Iago's own jealousy towards Cassio, who received the promotion Iago thought he deserved, sets the plot in motion.

2. **Manipulation and Deception**: The character of Iago embodies these themes. He manipulates others' perceptions and actions to create a false reality, eventually leading to the tragic downfall of Othello and others. His statement, "I am not what I am," highlights this theme of deceptive appearances.

3. **Race and Otherness**: The theme of race is a driving force in the plot of "Othello". The titular character is frequently referred to as 'the Moor', reminding the audience of his racial difference. This is often used in a derogatory way, for instance, when Brabantio accuses Othello of bewitching his daughter, saying, "Or with some mixtures powerful o'er the blood, Or with some dram conjured

to this effect, He wrought upon her."

4. **Love and Betrayal**: Love is a powerful force in the play, and it is seen in its most potent form in the relationship between Othello and Desdemona. However, their love is tragically destroyed by Iago's manipulation, resulting in a deep sense of betrayal. The destructive potential of love is demonstrated when Othello, consumed by jealousy, says, "Yet I'll not shed her blood; Nor scar that whiter skin of hers than snow, And smooth as monumental alabaster: yet she must die, else she'll betray more men."

5. **Identity and Reputation**: Reputation plays a significant role in the play. For Othello, the loss of his reputation, manipulated by Iago, is as devastating as the perceived loss of Desdemona's love. As he says, "O, I have lost my reputation! I have lost the immortal part of myself, and what remains is bestial."

6. **Gender**: Gender dynamics and the role of women in a patriarchal society are evident throughout the play. Desdemona, Emilia, and Bianca all face mistreatment or are undervalued in some form, reflecting the limited role and power of women in society.

Through these themes, Shakespeare creates a powerful narrative that invites readers and audiences to reflect on the human condition, its vulnerabilities, and its potential for both love and destruction.

CHARACTER ANALYSIS

Studying the characters in "Othello" provides insights into human psychology, motivation, and behavior. Each character in the play is complex, with their own strengths, weaknesses, desires, and fears.

1. **Othello**: Othello is a compelling character because he embodies both power and vulnerability. He is a respected military leader, yet his insecurities about his racial identity and his outsider status in Venetian society make him susceptible to manipulation. This is evident when Othello says, "Haply, for I am black, And have not those soft parts of conversation That chamberers have." His transformation from a loving husband to a jealous killer demonstrates the destructive power of jealousy and the tragic consequences of insecurity.

2. **Iago**: Iago is often considered one of literature's most sinister villains, yet his motivations are complex. His envy and resentment toward Othello and Cassio, as well as his possible suspicion about his wife's infidelity, drive his actions. Iago's ability to manipulate others reveals a keen understanding of human nature. He is a master of deceit, as demonstrated when he says, "I am not what I am."

3. **Desdemona**: Desdemona is a complex character who defies the gender norms of her time by marrying Othello against her father's

wishes and asserting her love for Othello in front of the Duke of Venice. However, her loyalty and trust in her husband, despite his increasingly irrational behavior, contribute to her tragic end. Desdemona's character provides an opportunity to explore themes of love, innocence, and the constraints of femininity in a patriarchal society.

4. **Emilia**: Emilia is Iago's wife and Desdemona's handmaid. She is an interesting character because she moves from being a passive observer to playing a crucial role in the tragic climax. Her realization of Iago's deception and her defiance against him serve as a commentary on the consequences of blind obedience and the power of truth.

5. **Cassio**: Cassio, whose promotion triggers Iago's revenge, is a loyal and competent soldier who values his reputation. His character provides a contrast to Othello's tragic downfall and serves to highlight Iago's manipulation.

By analyzing these characters and their interactions, students can delve into discussions about motives, morality, power dynamics, and the human condition. They can explore the ways in which personal flaws and societal pressures can lead to tragedy, a crucial aspect of understanding Shakespeare's tragedies and literature more generally.

— • —

LANGUAGE AND RHETORIC

"Othello" showcases Shakespeare's masterful use of language and rhetoric to develop character, convey emotion, and advance the plot. Here are some key elements:

1. **Imagery and Metaphor**: Shakespeare uses vivid imagery and metaphor throughout "Othello" to highlight the play's central themes. The image of the "green-eyed monster," for instance, personifies jealousy as a destructive and insatiable creature. The reference to Othello's "free and open nature" that Iago will use as his "net" underscores the danger of trust and openness when faced with deceit and manipulation.

2. **Animal Imagery**: Shakespeare frequently uses animal imagery to dehumanize Othello and express his perceived otherness. Iago refers to Othello and Desdemona's union as "an old black ram is tupping your white ewe," and later warns Brabantio that "your daughter and the Moor are now making the beast with two backs." This coarse animalistic language seeks to provoke disgust and fear and reflects the racial prejudices of the time.

3. **Irony**: Irony, both verbal and dramatic, is a key rhetorical tool in "Othello". Iago, the character who orchestrates much of the deception and conflict in the play, is repeatedly referred to as "honest Iago". This ongoing ironic reference underscores the dan-

gerous power of appearances and reputation. Dramatic irony is also employed, as the audience knows about Iago's deceitful plans while Othello and other characters do not.

4. **Soliloquy**: Soliloquies are used effectively in the play, particularly by Iago, to reveal motives and plans. For instance, Iago's soliloquy at the end of Act 1, where he outlines his plan to manipulate Othello's jealousy ("the Moor is of a free and open nature, that thinks men honest that but seem to be so, and will as tenderly be led by the nose as asses are") gives the audience insight into his manipulative character and sets the stage for the tragic events to follow.

5. **Prose and Verse**: The shift between prose and verse is used to differentiate characters and situations. Higher-status characters generally speak in verse (iambic pentameter), which is associated with nobility and formality, while lower-status characters or informal situations are often depicted in prose. Iago uses both, speaking in verse when he presents himself as loyal and honest, but switching to prose when he reveals his true intentions or manipulates others.

6. **Othello's Language**: Othello's language is significant in itself. In the early part of the play, Othello is eloquent and his speech is characterized by grand and romantic imagery, as when he describes his courtship of Desdemona ("She loved me for the dangers I had passed, And I loved her that she did pity them"). However, as jealousy takes hold, his speech becomes fragmented and disjointed, reflecting his emotional turmoil.

By studying the language and rhetoric in "Othello", students gain a deeper understanding of the play's themes, characters, and plot development, and also improve their understanding of English literature and linguistic styles more broadly.

UNDERSTANDING TRAGEDY

Understanding tragedy in relation to "Othello" involves examining the components that make this play a classic tragedy, consistent with Aristotle's definition: a play that results in a catastrophe, primarily the downfall of the protagonist, caused by a mistake or a character flaw. In "Othello", these elements of tragedy are clearly evident:

1. **Tragic Hero**: Othello, the protagonist, is the tragic hero. He is a man of high social status and respect, a successful military leader who is both noble and virtuous. However, as is typical in a tragedy, he has a tragic flaw, or 'hamartia', that leads to his downfall.

2. **Hamartia (Tragic Flaw)**: Othello's tragic flaw is his jealousy, but it is his insecurity about his outsider status that makes him susceptible to jealousy. Iago exploits this flaw masterfully, feeding Othello's jealousy with lies and insinuations until he is consumed by it. As Othello succumbs to jealousy, he says, "I'll see before I doubt; when I doubt, prove; and on the proof, there is no more but this: away at once with love or jealousy!"

3. **Peripeteia (Reversal of Fortune)**: Othello's status and fortune change dramatically over the course of the play. From a respected and successful general, happily married to Desdemona, he is reduced to a jealous and erratic man who kills his innocent wife and ends up taking his own life.

4. **Anagnorisis (Moment of Recognition)**: In a tragedy, the protagonist often has a moment of recognition, or 'anagnorisis', where they realize the truth that has been obscured by their tragic flaw. Othello's comes too late, after he has killed Desdemona, when Emilia reveals Iago's deceit. In despair, Othello laments, "O fool! fool! fool!" recognizing his own blindness and foolishness.

5. **Catharsis**: A tragedy is meant to invoke pity and fear in the audience, leading to a catharsis, or emotional purging. The audience feels pity for Othello's tragic downfall brought about by his own flaw, and fear recognizing the potential for similar flaws and errors in themselves.

Through these elements, "Othello" exemplifies the genre of tragedy. The understanding of tragedy is crucial to the analysis of the play, allowing readers to appreciate the narrative arc, the characters' actions and motivations, and the emotional impact of the story.

RELEVANCE TO CONTEMPORARY ISSUES

"Othello" is a play written over 400 years ago, but it remains relevant to contemporary issues and discussions. The themes Shakespeare explores resonate with many of the issues that society grapples with today. Here are some examples:

1. **Race and Otherness**: The play addresses the theme of racial prejudice, which is a pertinent issue in contemporary society. Othello's racial background and his status as an outsider are consistently highlighted in the play. The discrimination he faces and the insecurity he feels about his own identity resonate with the ongoing discussions about racial equality, representation, and the experiences of minority communities in predominantly white societies.

2. **Gender Dynamics and Misogyny**: "Othello" also explores the status and treatment of women in a patriarchal society. Desdemona, Emilia, and Bianca all experience mistreatment, ranging from Desdemona's murder to Emilia's verbal abuse and Bianca's objectification. These experiences connect with current discussions about gender equality, domestic violence, and the #MeToo movement.

3. **Manipulation and 'Fake News'**: Iago's manipulation of Othello, his exploitation of trust, and his creation of false narratives can

be paralleled with contemporary discussions about the power of misinformation and 'fake news'. It underscores the potential for damage when truth is distorted, which is relevant in today's era of digital media, where misinformation can spread quickly and broadly.

4. **Jealousy and Toxic Masculinity**: The destructive power of jealousy, as seen in Othello's actions, can be related to discussions about toxic masculinity and the harmful effects it can have on relationships and individuals. Othello's belief that violence and control are justified responses to Desdemona's perceived infidelity is a reflection of the harmful gender norms that persist in many societies today.

5. **Power and Corruption**: The play explores how power can be used and abused, as seen in Iago's actions. This can relate to discussions about ethical leadership, abuse of power, and the importance of accountability in contemporary society.

By studying "Othello", students can gain a historical perspective on these issues and understand how they have evolved over time. It can also provide a basis for meaningful discussion about these themes and their relevance to contemporary society.

— · —

RACE AND OTHERNESS THEME

The theme of race and otherness is one of the most significant aspects of "Othello". As a Moor in a predominantly white, Venetian society, Othello is an outsider, and this has a substantial impact on the events of the play and the perceptions of the characters.

1. **Otherness**: Throughout the play, Othello is constantly reminded of his otherness, both explicitly and subtly. This is first evidenced when Desdemona's father, Brabantio, accuses Othello of using magic to seduce Desdemona, suggesting that such a relationship is so unnatural that it could only be the result of enchantment. Brabantio's words, "Is there not charms By which the property of youth and maidhood May be abused?", reflects the racial prejudices of the time.

2. **Racial Prejudice**: Shakespeare portrays the racism Othello faces through the derogatory terms used to describe him, such as "thick-lips", "the devil", and "the blacker devil". This racism is not only verbal; it influences how people interpret Othello's actions. When Othello behaves rationally and calmly, his demeanor is seen as noble and dignified. But when he reacts with anger or jealousy, his behavior is attributed to his racial background, reinforcing damaging stereotypes.

3. **Internalized Racism**: Othello's outsider status and the racism

he faces also lead to self-doubt and insecurity. This internalized racism exacerbates Othello's jealousy and leads to his tragic downfall. His feelings of inferiority make him susceptible to Iago's insinuations about Desdemona's infidelity. The insecurity is evident in his words, "Haply, for I am black and have not those soft parts of conversation That chamberers have."

4. **Exploitation of Otherness**: Iago exploits Othello's otherness to manipulate him, using Othello's insecurity about his race and outsider status as a tool in his scheme. Iago's ability to plant seeds of doubt about Desdemona's fidelity is rooted in the societal belief that Desdemona, a white woman, wouldn't naturally be attracted to Othello.

In conclusion, the theme of race and otherness in "Othello" is a powerful commentary on the devastating impact of racism and prejudice. The play not only depicts the overt racism of the time but also shows how such prejudice can lead to internalized racism and be weaponized to manipulate others. This theme remains relevant to contemporary discussions about racial identity, prejudice, and the experiences of minority communities.

— · —

GENDER AND POWER

The exploration of gender and power dynamics is central to "Othello" and provides essential context for understanding literature and culture more broadly. The play explores traditional gender roles and the imbalance of power between genders in a patriarchal society. It also critiques these norms and provides insights into the harmful consequences of such inequality.

1. **Gender Roles**: Women in "Othello" are generally portrayed as passive, obedient, and subservient to men. However, Desdemona defies these norms by eloping with Othello, demonstrating agency and autonomy. Yet, her defiance is portrayed as a betrayal to her father, suggesting a societal expectation for women to be obedient and subservient. Desdemona says, "I am hitherto your daughter. But here's my husband. And so much duty as my mother showed to you, preferring you before her father, so much I challenge that I may profess due to the Moor my lord."

2. **Power Dynamics**: The power dynamics in "Othello" often revolve around gender. Men hold most of the power, and women are frequently viewed as possessions or objects. For example, Brabantio reacts to Desdemona's elopement as if he has been robbed of his property. Similarly, Othello feels that Desdemona's supposed infidelity has made him a cuckold, which he sees as damaging to his reputation and honor.

3. **Toxic Masculinity**: The play explores the damaging effects of toxic masculinity. Othello's sense of manhood is tied to his control over Desdemona. When he believes he has lost this control, he feels emasculated and reacts with violence, which ultimately leads to tragedy. This is evident when he says, "I'll tear her all to pieces," showing how his feelings of insecurity and emasculation drive his violent actions.

4. **Victimization of Women**: The women in "Othello" are victimized as a result of the patriarchal power structure. Desdemona is killed by her husband, Emilia is killed by her husband, and Bianca is wrongly accused and publicly shamed. Their experiences highlight the dangers and consequences of unchecked male power.

5. **Resistance and Subversion**: Despite their victimization, the female characters in the play also show resistance. Desdemona stands up for her love for Othello, Emilia exposes Iago's deceit, and Bianca defends herself against Cassio's dismissive treatment. These acts of resistance reflect a critique of the power dynamics of the time.

By studying these aspects of gender and power in "Othello", students can gain insights into historical gender norms and power dynamics, and how these norms have evolved over time. It can stimulate critical discussions about contemporary gender issues, the roots of these issues in historical norms, and the continued struggle for gender equality. The play serves as a platform to discuss and challenge the harmful consequences of gender inequality, making it a valuable text for studying literature and culture.

— · —

RELIGION AND CULTURE

The themes of religion and culture in "Othello" provide a valuable lens through which to study literature and culture. The play explores the intersection of different cultures and religions and the prejudices that arise from these differences.

1. **Cultural Clash**: As a Moor and a Muslim in Christian Venice, Othello embodies a cultural and religious clash. Othello's status as a cultural and religious outsider in Venetian society is a central element of the play. He is accepted for his military prowess but simultaneously "othered" due to his race and possibly his religion. This intersectionality is a rich subject for literary and cultural studies as it reveals a lot about societal attitudes and prejudices.

2. **Religious Imagery**: Religious imagery is used throughout the play to illuminate the moral and ethical dimensions of the characters' actions. For instance, Desdemona is often associated with religious purity, depicted as a "divine" and "heavenly" being. This sanctification enhances the horror of Othello's decision to murder her. It also underscores the societal expectation of female purity and innocence in this religious context.

3. **Cultural Prejudices**: The play highlights the cultural prejudices that existed in Elizabethan society. Othello's 'otherness' is emphasized through his different race, culture, and possibly religion,

which contributes to his marginalization. This theme is very relevant to modern discussions about cultural identity, xenophobia, and the experiences of immigrants or minorities.

4. **Religious Conversion**: It's possible that Othello converted to Christianity, as was common for many Moors living in Christian societies at that time. If this is the case, Othello's story reflects the complexities of religious conversion and assimilation. He might be grappling with the tension of maintaining his original cultural identity while integrating into a different religious and cultural context.

In the context of studying literature and culture, "Othello" offers insights into how religion and culture shape identities, societal norms, and interpersonal relationships. It invites discussions about prejudice, assimilation, and cultural clash, topics that resonate with contemporary issues of multiculturalism, religious tolerance, and cultural diversity. It helps students understand historical attitudes towards religion and culture and trace their evolution over time. The themes of religion and culture in "Othello" also shed light on the complex interplay of personal, societal, and religious forces in shaping individuals' actions and societal outcomes.

SOCIAL HIERARCHY AND MILITARY CULTURE

"Othello" provides a robust exploration of social hierarchy and military culture, particularly as it pertains to the Elizabethan period. The study of these themes is essential to fully understanding the narrative and cultural implications of the play.

1. **Social Hierarchy**: Venetian society, like many societies of the time, was heavily stratified. People were expected to know their place and behave according to their class. Othello's status as a military leader places him near the top of the hierarchy, yet his racial background creates a paradoxical position of power and inferiority. This dichotomy is highlighted in the reactions to Othello's marriage to Desdemona, who is from a higher social class due to her familial connections. Their union disrupts the social order, causing tension and conflict. When Othello marries Desdemona, Brabantio says, "She, in spite of nature, Of years, of country, credit, everything, To fall in love with what she feared to look on!"

2. **Military Culture**: Othello is not just a Moor; he is a military general. His identity and status are intertwined with his military role, affecting his relationships and actions throughout the play. The military culture, marked by a strict chain of command, honor, and discipline, shapes Othello's worldview and decision-making. It also sets up a dynamic where obedience and loyalty are paramount. This aspect is exploited by Iago, a lower-ranking officer

who uses his perceived loyalty to deceive Othello.

3. **Social Mobility through Military Success**: Othello's rise to power as a general, despite being a foreigner and a racial outsider, reflects the possibility of social mobility through military success. However, it also underscores the precariousness of this position, as Othello's acceptance in Venetian society is conditional and contingent on his military usefulness. Once his judgment is perceived as flawed, his outsider status becomes more pronounced.

4. **Honour and Reputation**: In the military and social hierarchy, honour and reputation are crucial. Othello's downfall is precipitated by his fear of losing his honor and reputation due to Desdemona's supposed infidelity. This is evidenced in his statement, "For I am black, And have not those soft parts of conversation That chamberers have; or for I am declined into the vale of years—yet that's not much— She's gone."

The exploration of social hierarchy and military culture in "Othello" illuminates the complexities of social status, power dynamics, and the role of institutions in shaping identity and relationships. It provides a framework for discussing issues of class, race, power, and how they intersect with institutional cultures. The play serves as a critique of the rigid social hierarchies and military values of the time, making it an important text for studying literature and culture.

— · —

MANIPULATION AND DECEPTION

Manipulation and deception form the very crux of "Othello". The unfolding of these themes through the character of Iago provides fascinating insight into the psychological aspects of human behaviour. It shows how manipulation and deception can lead to disastrous consequences, making it a valuable subject of study in literature and culture.

1. **Iago's Manipulation**: Iago, the character at the center of the play's deception, manipulates virtually every other character. His tactics reveal a deep understanding of human nature and vulnerability, which he uses to bend others to his will. An example of this manipulation can be seen when he warns Othello of jealousy, saying "O, beware, my lord, of jealousy; It is the green-ey'd monster, which doth mock The meat it feeds on." He plants the seeds of doubt in Othello's mind, leading him towards destructive jealousy.

2. **Deception as a Tool**: The theme of deception is a powerful tool that Shakespeare uses to advance the plot and develop characters. Almost all of Iago's interactions are deceptive, as he presents himself as honest and loyal while orchestrating events for his benefit. His ability to "wear many masks" is an important element of his character and the plot. His self-description encapsulates this: "I am not what I am."

3. **Effects of Deception**: The play examines the consequences of deception, which range from jealousy and mistrust to death and destruction. The destructive power of lies is demonstrated when Othello, consumed by Iago's false information, ends up killing Desdemona and then himself. This is highlighted in Othello's lament: "Why did I marry? This honest creature doubtless Sees and knows more, much more, than he unfolds."

4. **Psychology of Deception**: Othello provides a detailed study of the psychology of deception. It explores how deception can manipulate perception and lead to irrational actions. It examines the factors that make individuals vulnerable to deception, such as Othello's insecurity about his outsider status and Desdemona's innocence.

5. **Role of Trust**: The play also explores the role of trust in manipulation and deception. Othello's trust in the seemingly honest Iago leads him astray, illustrating how trust can be exploited for deceptive purposes.

In the context of studying literature and culture, "Othello" provides insights into the human capacity for deception and the vulnerability of trust. It sheds light on the psychological, emotional, and societal effects of manipulation and deception, topics that remain relevant in contemporary societal and cultural studies. It can foster discussions about the ethics of deception, the dynamics of trust, and the psychological factors that influence vulnerability to manipulation. Thus, the themes of manipulation and deception in "Othello" have lasting relevance and value in the study of literature and culture.

Jealousy theme

Jealousy is one of the most prominent themes in "Othello". Often referred to as the "green-eyed monster" in the play, jealousy is the driving force behind the tragic events in the story.

1. **Othello's Jealousy**: The most devastating example of jealousy is that of Othello. Driven by Iago's insinuations and false evidence, Othello becomes intensely jealous of his faithful wife, Desdemona. He believes she has been unfaithful to him with Cassio, even though there is no credible evidence of this. Consumed by his jealousy, Othello transforms from a composed and loving husband into a vengeful murderer. He confesses, "I had been happy if the general camp, Pioners and all, had tasted her sweet body, So I had nothing known. O, now, for ever Farewell the tranquil mind! Farewell content!" These lines reveal the all-consuming nature of his jealousy that overpowers his previously rational mind.

2. **Iago's Jealousy**: Iago's manipulation of Othello stems from his own jealousy. He is envious of Cassio for receiving the promotion he thought he deserved, and he is suspicious that Othello may have slept with his wife, Emilia. Iago says, "I hate the Moor, And it is thought abroad that 'twixt my sheets He's done my office. I know not if 't be true, But I, for mere suspicion in that kind, Will do as if for surety."

3. **Roderigo's Jealousy**: Roderigo is jealous of Othello for marrying Desdemona, whom he passionately loves. Iago uses Roderigo's jealousy to manipulate him into doing his bidding, thereby setting the plot in motion.

4. **The Destructive Power of Jealousy**: The play shows that jealousy, once planted, grows and overshadows all other emotions. It can cause people to abandon their judgement, as seen with Othello, and it can lead to destructive actions, as seen with all the major characters influenced by jealousy.

5. **The Manipulation of Jealousy**: Iago is a master manipulator who uses others' jealousy for his ends. He understands the destructive power of jealousy and wields it as a weapon, demonstrating how easily human emotions can be manipulated to lead to downfall.

The theme of jealousy in "Othello" provides a deep exploration of the darker side of human emotions. It shows how unchecked jealousy can lead to mistrust, miscommunication, and, ultimately, tragic outcomes. It presents jealousy as a powerful and destructive force that can warp reality and drive individuals to act against their best interests. By studying this theme, students can gain valuable insights into human emotions, their susceptibility to manipulation, and their potential to lead to tragic consequences.

— · —

MANIPULATION AND DESCEPTION THEME

Manipulation and deception form the core of Shakespeare's "Othello". These themes drive the plot forward and provide a basis for character development, particularly in the character of Iago, whose expert manipulation and deception lead to the tragic downfall of Othello.

1. **Iago's Manipulation and Deception**: Iago, the antagonist of the play, is the chief manipulator and deceiver. His cunning and deceitful nature allow him to manipulate the other characters towards his own ends. His words to Roderigo perfectly encapsulate his deceitful nature: "I follow him [Othello] to serve my turn upon him."

2. **Deception as a Tool**: Iago uses deception as a tool, constructing lies and half-truths to incite doubt and jealousy in Othello. A notable instance of this is when Iago convinces Othello that his wife, Desdemona, has been unfaithful with Cassio. This is achieved through the careful orchestration of events and manipulative dialogues, as when he warns Othello of jealousy: "O, beware, my lord, of jealousy; It is the green-eyed monster which doth mock the meat it feeds on."

3. **Effects of Manipulation and Deception**: The effects of Iago's manipulation and deception are catastrophic, leading to the unraveling of Othello's life. His trust in Iago and belief in his lies

result in the tragic death of Desdemona, and ultimately, his own suicide. This is underscored by Othello's lament: "O fool! fool! fool!"

4. **Manipulation of Trust**: Trust and its exploitation form a major part of the play's exploration of manipulation and deception. Iago uses his reputation for honesty and loyalty to manipulate others, highlighting the theme of appearance versus reality. This is epitomized in his statement: "I am not what I am."

5. **Impact on Relationships**: Manipulation and deception also have a profound impact on the relationships in the play. The mistrust sown by Iago leads to the breakdown of Othello's relationship with Desdemona, and even causes fractures in Iago's relationship with his wife, Emilia.

The themes of manipulation and deception in "Othello" offer a deep exploration of human vice and vulnerability. They reveal the devastating impact of deceit and manipulation on individuals and relationships. Studying these themes can provide valuable insights into human psychology, ethics, and social relationships. They highlight the potential for trust to be exploited and the tragic consequences that can arise from manipulation and deception.

— · —

RACE AND OTHERNESS THEME

"Othello" is one of Shakespeare's most complex plays, with themes of race and otherness playing a significant role. Othello, the protagonist, is a Moor living in a predominantly white society. His "otherness" influences how other characters perceive and interact with him, shaping the play's tragic course.

1. **Othello's Otherness**: Othello's racial and cultural difference is evident from the start. The derogatory term "the Moor," used to describe him, underscores his outsider status. For instance, when Iago informs Desdemona's father Brabantio of her marriage to Othello, he refers to Othello as "an old black ram," a racialized and offensive description.

2. **Race and Perception**: Othello's race not only sets him apart but also influences how others perceive him. Despite his high military rank, Othello is subjected to racist attitudes. When Brabantio discovers Desdemona's marriage to Othello, he accuses Othello of using witchcraft, unable to believe that his daughter could willingly choose to marry someone of a different race: "She's deceived by witchcraft."

3. **Race and Power**: Othello's status as a respected military general in a white society is a notable element in the play. However, his power is precarious, contingent upon his military success and his

ability to conform to Venetian norms. When he's perceived to have lost his rationality due to jealousy, his race is quickly used against him, reinforcing his status as the "other."

4. **Race and Identity**: Othello's identity is strongly tied to his race, affecting his self-perception and sense of belonging. His insecurity about his racial otherness is one reason he falls so readily for Iago's deception about Desdemona's infidelity. He expresses his fear and sense of otherness in Act 3, Scene 3: "Haply, for I am black and have not those soft parts of conversation that chamberers have, or for I am declined into the vale of years..."

5. **Otherness as a Tool of Manipulation**: Iago manipulates Othello's sense of otherness to incite his jealousy and ultimately bring about his downfall. By making Othello feel alienated and isolated, Iago can more easily control him and set him on the path to destruction.

Through the themes of race and otherness, "Othello" provides a critical examination of racial dynamics and othering in society. This exploration is relevant for contemporary discussions around race, otherness, and power dynamics in multicultural societies. It presents a profound study of how these factors can affect individuals' sense of self and their interactions with others, and how they can be manipulated for malicious ends.

— · —

LOVE AND BETRAYAL THEME

"Othello" explores the themes of love and betrayal in profound depth. These two intertwined themes form the heart of the tragedy, revealing the characters' vulnerabilities and driving the plot towards its tragic climax.

1. **Love**: The love between Othello and Desdemona initiates the action of the play. Desdemona defies societal norms and her father to marry Othello, a foreigner. Othello, in turn, is deeply in love with Desdemona, which is evident in his speeches about her: "She loved me for the dangers I had passed, And I loved her that she did pity them."

2. **Betrayal**: Betrayal, real or perceived, also pervades the play. Iago feels betrayed by Othello when he promotes Cassio over him. This sense of betrayal drives Iago to plot against Othello, showing how perceived slights can breed destructive actions: "In following him, I follow but myself; Heaven is my judge, not I for love and duty, But seeming so, for my peculiar end."

3. **Love Turned Into Betrayal**: Othello's love for Desdemona becomes a source of his own undoing. As Iago manipulates Othello into believing that Desdemona has been unfaithful, Othello's love morphs into a destructive force. He feels betrayed by the woman he loves, resulting in him strangling Desdemona: "Yet she must die, else she'll betray more men."

4. **Betrayal of Trust**: The theme of trust and its betrayal is intricately woven with love and betrayal. Othello trusts Iago implicitly, referring to him as "honest Iago," and it is this trust that Iago manipulates to deceive Othello and drive him to murderous jealousy.

5. **Self-Betrayal**: Othello's acceptance of Iago's lies also constitutes a self-betrayal. He abandons his judgement, allowing jealousy to cloud his love for Desdemona, which ultimately leads to his downfall: "O, the world hath not a sweeter creature! She might lie by an emperor's side and command him tasks."

The themes of love and betrayal in "Othello" provide a profound exploration of human emotions and their vulnerability to manipulation. They show the fragility of love in the face of jealousy and suspicion, and how trust can be exploited and turned into a weapon of betrayal. By studying these themes, students can gain valuable insights into the complexities of human relationships, the destructive power of jealousy, and the tragic consequences of betrayal.

— · —

IDENTITY AND REPUTATION THEME

In "Othello", the themes of identity and reputation play crucial roles in the development of the plot and characters. They drive the motivations of characters, influence perceptions and relationships, and ultimately, lead to the tragedy.

1. **Othello's Reputation**: Othello's identity as a valiant soldier and his reputation as a competent military leader are what earn him respect and admiration in Venetian society, despite his status as a racial and cultural outsider. He is able to win Desdemona's love because of his "honours and valiant parts" (Act 1, Scene 3).

2. **Iago's Reputation**: Iago's reputation for honesty and loyalty is crucial to his manipulation of others. Despite his villainous intentions, he is regarded as "Honest Iago" by other characters. He manipulates this reputation to his advantage, allowing him to deceive others without arousing suspicion.

3. **Cassio's Reputation**: Cassio's reputation is an important aspect of the play. When he loses his position as Othello's lieutenant due to his drunken behavior, he is desperate to restore his reputation, which he considers to be his "immediate jewel" (Act 2, Scene 3). Iago exploits Cassio's concern for his reputation to further his own schemes.

4. **Reputation and Identity**: The characters' perceptions of their

own identities are closely tied to their reputations. Othello's sense of self-worth begins to deteriorate when he believes that his wife, Desdemona, has been unfaithful to him. He perceives her alleged infidelity as a direct stain on his reputation and identity, leading him to tragic actions.

5. **Identity as an Outsider**: Othello's identity as an outsider is a central theme in the play. Despite his success and high status, he never fully escapes his sense of otherness, often referring to himself as one who "loved not wisely but too well" (Act 5, Scene 2). His identity as an outsider is further manipulated by Iago to breed suspicion and jealousy, leading to his downfall.

In "Othello", the themes of identity and reputation reveal how personal and social perceptions can influence actions, relationships, and fate. These themes are a rich source of discussion about individual identity, societal values, and the fragile nature of reputation. Studying them can provide valuable insights into the influence of external perceptions on self-perception, and the potentially tragic consequences of a damaged reputation.

— · —

GENDER THEME

In "Othello", Shakespeare explores the theme of gender through the experiences and interactions of the characters, particularly in terms of the roles and expectations of women during the Elizabethan era.

1. **Desdemona**: Desdemona challenges societal norms by choosing to marry Othello of her own accord, defying her father in the process: "To you I am bound for life and education; My life and education both do learn me How to respect you...But here's my husband" (Act 1, Scene 3). However, her obedience and loyalty to Othello ultimately leads to her downfall, reflecting the vulnerability of women in a male-dominated society.

2. **Emilia**: Emilia also provides insights into gender roles. She is initially submissive to her husband Iago, assisting him in his scheme against Othello. However, she eventually stands against him, revealing his deceit and vindicating Desdemona: "I will not charm my tongue; I am bound to speak" (Act 5, Scene 2). This transformation depicts a shift in gender dynamics.

3. **Patriarchy and Power**: The play explores patriarchal power structures. Men are shown to dominate the public sphere, holding positions of power and control, while women are relegated to the private sphere. Othello's tragic decision to murder Desdemona is a result of male dominance and jealousy: "Put out the light, and

then put out the light." (Act 5, Scene 2)

4. **Objectification of Women**: Women are frequently objectified and treated as possessions. For instance, Brabantio views Desdemona as his property, expressing outrage when she is "stolen" by Othello: "O thou foul thief, where hast thou stowed my daughter?" (Act 1, Scene 2).

5. **Women's Voice and Silence**: Desdemona's voice is silenced both metaphorically and literally when she is murdered by Othello, showcasing the lack of agency women had in society. Even Emilia's revelations about Iago's villainy come too late to save Desdemona, underlining the tragic consequences of women's voices being ignored or suppressed.

Studying the theme of gender in "Othello" offers important insights into gender dynamics and the societal structures of Shakespeare's time. The play raises questions about women's agency, the effects of patriarchal power, and the objectification of women. It remains relevant today, as society continues to grapple with these issues of gender and power.

IMAGERY AND METAPHOR

"Othello" is rich in imagery and metaphors that enhance its dramatic impact and provide insight into characters' emotions, motivations, and perceptions. Shakespeare masterfully uses these literary devices to make abstract ideas tangible and to convey the emotional intensity of the plot.

1. **Animal Imagery**: One of the most persistent uses of imagery in "Othello" is animal imagery, primarily used by Iago to dehumanize Othello and make his relationship with Desdemona seem unnatural. Iago uses crude animalistic metaphors when he informs Brabantio about Desdemona's elopement, saying that "an old black ram / Is tupping your white ewe" (Act 1, Scene 1). This degrading imagery reveals Iago's racism and his intention to provoke Brabantio.

2. **Hell and Devil Imagery**: Imagery related to the devil and hell is also prevalent, often used to describe or refer to Othello. Iago manipulates Othello's emotions, using such imagery to incite his jealousy: "O, beware, my lord, of jealousy; / It is the green-eyed monster which doth mock / The meat it feeds on" (Act 3, Scene 3). Such references heighten the sense of Othello's internal torment.

3. **Imagery of Light and Darkness**: Shakespeare also employs the imagery of light and darkness to represent purity and corrup-

tion, love and jealousy. When Othello succumbs to jealousy, he declares, "Her name, that was as fresh / As Dian's visage, is now begrimed and black / As mine own face" (Act 3, Scene 3). The contrast between "fresh" and "begrimed and black" reflects Othello's changing perception of Desdemona, influenced by Iago's insinuations.

4. **Poison and Disease Imagery**: Poison and disease imagery is used to symbolize the destructive power of jealousy and deceit. Iago is often the source of this imagery, likening his own manipulations to poison: "I'll pour this pestilence into his ear" (Act 2, Scene 3). This metaphor enhances our understanding of Iago's malevolence and the destructive nature of his lies.

5. **Garden and Weed Imagery**: The garden and weed metaphor is used to illustrate how unchecked jealousy can grow and destroy. When Iago plants the seeds of doubt about Desdemona's fidelity in Othello's mind, he says, "And will as tenderly be led by th' nose / As asses are. / I have't. It is engendered. Hell and night / Must bring this monstrous birth to the world's light" (Act 1, Scene 3). The imagery here underscores the manipulative strategy of Iago and the ruinous consequences that are to follow.

Through the use of vivid and complex imagery and metaphor, Shakespeare crafts a compelling narrative filled with tension, emotion, and depth. These literary devices not only provide a more profound understanding of the characters but also allow audiences to grasp the psychological and emotional undercurrents of the play. Analyzing this rich use of language and rhetoric can greatly enhance the reading and interpretation of "Othello".

— · —

ANIMAL IMAGERY

Shakespeare employs animal imagery to great effect, using it to enhance characterization, reveal prejudices, and symbolize the baser aspects of human nature.

1. **Dehumanizing Othello**: Iago frequently uses animal imagery to dehumanize Othello, making his relationship with Desdemona appear unnatural. For instance, Iago incites Brabantio by crudely informing him of Desdemona's elopement with Othello: "an old black ram / Is tupping your white ewe" (Act 1, Scene 1). Here, the imagery reduces Othello and Desdemona to beasts, playing into Brabantio's fears and racial prejudices.

2. **Iago's Manipulative Nature**: Animal imagery also provides insight into Iago's manipulative character. He likens his deceitful instigation of Othello's jealousy to hunting: "I will, in Cassio's lodging, lose this napkin / And let him find it. Trifles light as air / Are to the jealous confirmations strong / As proofs of holy writ: this may do something" (Act 3, Scene 3). The imagery here conveys his strategic, predator-like approach.

3. **Othello's Transformation**: Othello, initially portrayed as a noble figure, undergoes a transformation under the influence of Iago's machinations. The more Othello succumbs to jealousy, the more he uses animal imagery, suggesting a regression into a more

primal state. When his jealousy peaks, Othello growls, "Arise, black vengeance, from thy hollow cell! / Yield up, O love, thy crown and hearted throne / To tyrannous hate!" (Act 3, Scene 3). Here, the animalistic 'black vengeance' shows how his nobility has been overshadowed by raw, destructive emotion.

4. **Symbol of Uncontrolled Passions**: Animal imagery in "Othello" frequently symbolizes uncontrolled passions, instincts, and destructive behaviors. For example, when Iago wants to encourage Othello's jealousy, he warns him about the "green-eyed monster" (Act 3, Scene 3). The 'monster' metaphorically represents jealousy as a wild, uncontrollable creature that can consume and destroy its host.

5. **Desdemona's Innocence**: In contrast to the aggressive, predatory animal imagery associated with male characters, Desdemona is associated with imagery of innocent, docile animals. When Othello is about to murder her, he likens her to a "rose" and a "young and rose-lipped cherubin" (Act 5, Scene 2), emphasizing her innocence and his extreme act of cruelty.

In conclusion, Shakespeare's use of animal imagery in "Othello" amplifies the intensity of emotions, highlights racial prejudices, and reveals character depths. This vivid and often disturbing imagery serves as a critical component of the play's language and rhetoric, illustrating the tragedy of noble characters succumbing to their basest instincts.

IRONY

Irony is a powerful tool that Shakespeare uses frequently in "Othello" to enhance the tragic elements and depth of the narrative. It adds a layer of complexity to the language and rhetoric, serving to underscore character traits, reveal dramatic truths, and intensify the play's emotional impact.

1. **Dramatic Irony**: Dramatic irony, where the audience knows something that the characters do not, is prevalent throughout the play. One of the most significant instances occurs when Othello believes Iago's lies about Desdemona's infidelity. The audience, privy to Iago's manipulations, watches as Othello is misled, increasing the sense of tragedy: "O, beware, my lord, of jealousy; / It is the green-eyed monster which doth mock / The meat it feeds on" (Act 3, Scene 3).

2. **Situational Irony**: Situational irony, where events do not turn out as expected, is also used effectively. Desdemona's handkerchief, a token of love from Othello, becomes twisted into "evidence" of her unfaithfulness. The handkerchief, meant to symbolize love and fidelity, ironically fuels Othello's destructive jealousy.

3. **Verbal Irony**: Verbal irony, where a character says one thing but means another, is most often found in Iago's dialogue. He frequently pretends to be concerned for others while scheming

against them, such as when he warns Othello about the dangers of jealousy while stoking it: "I speak not yet of proof. / Look to your wife; observe her well with Cassio" (Act 3, Scene 3).

4. **Irony of Character**: The irony also extends to the characterization. Iago, the villain, is repeatedly referred to as "honest Iago", highlighting the stark contrast between how characters perceive him and his true deceitful nature. Similarly, Othello, a respected and noble military leader, is driven to the basest of actions - murder - due to his misplaced trust in Iago.

5. **Irony in the Tragic Ending**: The tragic irony of the play culminates in its final act. Othello kills Desdemona to protect his honor, only to discover that she was innocent all along. His realization of the truth, "this look of thine will hurl my soul from heaven, / And fiends will snatch at it" (Act 5, Scene 2), underscores the tragic irony of his actions based on a lie.

Through the use of irony, "Othello" presents a multifaceted exploration of manipulation, trust, and deception. The frequent ironic contrasts between appearance and reality contribute significantly to the play's tragic tension and emotional depth. Thus, understanding the role of irony can significantly enhance one's appreciation of the play's language, rhetoric, and thematic complexity.

SOLILOQUY

In "Othello," as in many of his plays, Shakespeare makes powerful use of the soliloquy—a speech delivered by a character when they are alone, intended to reveal their innermost thoughts and emotions. These soliloquies offer the audience intimate access to a character's mind, heightening dramatic tension and revealing hidden aspects of their character.

1. **Iago's Soliloquies**: Iago's soliloquies are some of the most revealing and important in the play. For example, in Act 1, Scene 3, Iago reveals his plans to manipulate Othello and Cassio: "After some time, to abuse Othello's ear / That he is too familiar with his wife." His soliloquies give the audience insight into his malevolent intentions, enhancing the dramatic irony since the audience knows more about Iago's intentions than the other characters do.

2. **Othello's Soliloquies**: Othello's soliloquies offer an insight into his transformation from a noble general to a jealous husband. In Act 3, Scene 3, Othello says, "Why did I marry? This honest creature doubtless / Sees and knows more, much more, than he unfolds." This soliloquy shows the audience his growing suspicion towards Desdemona, highlighting the success of Iago's manipulations. Later, in Act 5, Scene 2, before he kills Desdemona, he delivers another soliloquy that showcases his internal struggle and the tragic climax of his jealousy.

3. **Language and Rhetoric**: The soliloquies in "Othello" are characterized by vivid imagery and powerful rhetorical devices, intensifying their emotional impact. Iago's soliloquies often feature cynical and crude imagery that reflects his twisted nature, while Othello's soliloquies become increasingly troubled and conflicted as the play progresses.

4. **Foreshadowing**: Soliloquies are often used to foreshadow future events in the play. In Act 2, Scene 1, Iago's soliloquy hints at the tragic conclusion: "Knavery's plain face is never seen till used." This hints at his manipulative scheme, subtly foreshadowing the disastrous events to follow.

5. **Exposition and Plot Advancement**: Soliloquies are also used for exposition and to advance the plot. They reveal motivations, plans, and feelings that drive the actions of the characters. For instance, Iago's soliloquies map out his scheming and reveal the depth of his villainy, which are critical to the unfolding tragedy.

By analyzing the soliloquies in "Othello," readers can gain deeper insight into the characters and their motivations. They're an integral part of the play's language and rhetoric, adding layers of complexity to the characters and enhancing the dramatic impact of the plot.

— · —

PROSE AND VERSE

Shakespeare's "Othello" uses a mixture of verse and prose, providing a variety of rhetorical effects that both inform the audience about the characters and enhance the drama. This deliberate use of language reveals insights into the characters' status, their emotions, and the tone of the scene.

1. **Verse**: Verse, often in the form of iambic pentameter, is used frequently by Shakespeare in "Othello," particularly in formal, emotional, or dramatic contexts. High-ranking characters like Othello or nobility typically speak in verse. When Othello defends himself to the Venetian senators against the accusations of witchcraft, he speaks in blank verse: "Her father loved me; oft invited me; / Still questioned me the story of my life / From year to year, the battles, sieges, fortunes" (Act 1, Scene 3). This lends dignity and formality to his speech.

2. **Prose**: Prose is used for ordinary conversation or for comic effect. Lower-status characters often speak in prose, indicating their social standing. Characters might also use prose to disguise their true intentions or to manipulate others. Iago, for instance, often uses prose when he is plotting or manipulating. In Act 1, Scene 3, he speaks in prose to Roderigo, outlining his deceitful plan: "I follow him to serve my turn upon him." The shift to prose here also signals Iago's duplicity, as he drops the formal verse to reveal his true nature.

3. **Switching Between Prose and Verse**: The transition between verse and prose can highlight changes in a character's emotional state or the tone of the scene. For example, Othello often speaks in verse, reflecting his status and composure, but as he succumbs to Iago's manipulation, he descends into prose, indicating his emotional upheaval. In Act 4, Scene 1, upon hearing of Desdemona's alleged unfaithfulness, Othello falls into a trance, exclaiming in prose, "Lie with her? Lie on her? We say lie on her when they belie her! Lie with her—that's fulsome. Handkerchief—confessions—handkerchief! To confess and be hanged for his labor."

Shakespeare's alternation between verse and prose allows for a dynamic exploration of the characters and their emotional states. It also creates contrast between scenes, helps emphasize dramatic moments, and gives a rhythmic and musical quality to the dialogue. These features of language and rhetoric, specific to each character and scene, greatly enhance the dramatic effect of "Othello."

— • —

OTHELLO'S LANGUAGE

The language used by Othello in Shakespeare's play is a key element in understanding his character, and it undergoes significant changes as the play progresses. His speech is characterized by its eloquence, dignity, and, as he descends into jealousy and madness, an increasing agitation and incoherence.

1. **Eloquence and Dignity**: Othello initially speaks in an eloquent and dignified manner, reflecting his position as a respected military leader. His verse is often formal, measured, and filled with grand and noble imagery, especially when describing his experiences or defending his love for Desdemona. For instance, in Act 1, Scene 3, he explains his wooing of Desdemona: "She loved me for the dangers I had passed, / And I loved her that she did pity them". This showcases his noble nature and his ability to express himself eloquently.

2. **Imagery and Metaphor**: Othello often uses powerful, vivid imagery and metaphors in his speech, particularly when he's expressing his strong emotions. In Act 3, Scene 3, Othello's despair at Desdemona's perceived infidelity is illustrated with a potent metaphor: "Oh, now, forever / Farewell the tranquil mind! Farewell content! / Farewell the plumèd troops and the big wars / That make ambition virtue!"

3. **Transition to Agitated Prose**: As Iago's manipulation takes hold and Othello's jealousy inflames, his language deteriorates from the calm, measured verse into fragmented, agitated prose, symbolizing his emotional turmoil and descent into madness. In Act 4, Scene 1, he rambles incoherently about the handkerchief, a symbol of Desdemona's alleged infidelity: "Handkerchief—confessions—handkerchief!—". His previously eloquent speech is reduced to broken phrases, reflecting his mental state.

4. **Influence of Iago's Language**: It is important to note the influence of Iago's language on Othello. Iago's language is poisonous and manipulative, filled with insinuations and vile imagery. This starts to permeate Othello's speech as he succumbs to jealousy. He begins to echo Iago's animalistic, crude language, as shown when he refers to his wife with terms like "goat" and "monkey" in Act 3, Scene 3: "I'll tear her all to pieces!".

In "Othello," the title character's language not only reveals his mental and emotional state but also the play's progression from order to chaos. The transformation of Othello's language from eloquent verse to fragmented prose is a stark reflection of his tragic downfall. It adds depth to his character and intensifies the play's dramatic tension. Understanding this shift in Othello's speech is crucial for a comprehensive appreciation of the play's language and rhetoric.

Tragic Hero

In literature, a tragic hero is a protagonist who experiences a significant downfall due to their own tragic flaw and the consequences of their choices. In "Othello," the character of Othello fits this mold, following a trajectory that fulfills several key characteristics of the tragic hero archetype, based on Aristotle's concept of tragedy.

1. **Noble Stature**: Tragic heroes are typically individuals of high rank or status, and their downfall often has widespread repercussions. Othello, as a respected general in the Venetian army, fulfills this criterion. His fall from grace results in multiple deaths and the loss of trust within the Venetian society.

2. **Tragic Flaw (Hamartia)**: The tragic hero's downfall is often precipitated by a personal failing, known as a tragic flaw. In Othello's case, his tragic flaw is his jealousy and his inherent trust in Iago. Iago manipulates these traits, using Othello's love for Desdemona and his trust in Iago's honesty to plant seeds of doubt about Desdemona's fidelity.

3. **Reversal of Fortune (Peripeteia)**: Tragic heroes experience a reversal in fortune, where their high status is dramatically flipped into a low state. Othello, once a respected and successful military leader, becomes a murderer and an outcast due to his actions resulting from jealousy.

4. **Recognition (Anagnorisis)**: Often, the tragic hero has a moment of recognition or self-awareness, where they understand the nature of their error and its impact. In Act 5, Scene 2, Othello realizes the truth of Desdemona's innocence and Iago's deceit: "O fool! fool! fool!" This moment of self-realization, however, comes too late to prevent the tragic outcome.

5. **Catharsis**: The audience should experience catharsis—a purging or cleansing of emotion—at the end of the play. Othello's death, while tragic, serves as a kind of release from the tension built up over the course of the play. His suicide, while certainly not condoned, demonstrates his deep remorse and guilt over his actions: "I kissed thee ere I killed thee. No way but this, / Killing myself, to die upon a kiss" (Act 5, Scene 2).

In these ways, Othello is a tragic hero whose downfall is brought about by a combination of his own tragic flaw and Iago's manipulation. His journey from a respected general to a jealous murderer exemplifies the essence of a tragic hero, and his story ultimately serves as a cautionary tale about the destructive potential of unchecked jealousy. The audience's understanding of Othello as a tragic hero is crucial to interpreting the tragic impact and themes of the play.

— · —

RACE AND OTHERNESS

"Othello," written by William Shakespeare in the early 17th century, remains relevant in its exploration of race and otherness – themes that continue to resonate today. As one of the few Shakespearean characters explicitly identified as a person of color, Othello's experiences offer a lens to examine racial bias, identity, and the experience of being an outsider.

Racial Identity and Bias

Shakespeare represents Othello as a Moor, a term historically used to describe individuals from the North African region. The significance of this racial identity lies in the character's noble status – he is a highly respected military general, countering contemporary European assumptions of racial superiority. However, his achievements do not protect him from racial bias, as seen through derogatory racial slurs, such as "thick-lips" (Act 1, Scene 1) or "black ram" (Act 1, Scene 1), suggesting a dehumanizing and animalistic perception of him. His race is also weaponized against him when Brabantio accuses him of witchcraft, exploiting prevalent stereotypes about black magic and racial 'otherness': "Thou hast enchanted her; / For I'll refer me to all things of sense, / If she in chains of magic were not bound," (Act 1, Scene 2).

Otherness and Alienation

Despite his high status and the respect commanded through his military accomplishments, Othello remains an outsider in Venetian society due to his race and cultural background. His 'otherness' is continuously highlighted, particularly in his relationship with Desdemona. When Iago manipulates Othello into believing that Desdemona has been unfaithful, he plays on Othello's insecurities about being an outsider, "I know our country disposition well; / In Venice they do let heaven see the pranks / They dare not show their husbands." (Act 3, Scene 3). This reinforces the perception that Othello will never truly belong or be accepted in Venetian society.

Contemporary Relevance

These themes of race and otherness remain as relevant today as when Shakespeare penned "Othello." In many societies, racial bias continues to persist, and those seen as 'different' or 'other' still often face discrimination and prejudice. Recent movements, such as Black Lives Matter, underscore the ongoing struggle against systemic racism and the urgency of addressing these issues.

In the face of racial bias, Othello's fall from grace can be interpreted as an exploration of the psychological effects of racism and societal exclusion. His tragic end can be viewed as a critique of a society that marginalizes and alienates based on race, resulting in the victim's self-destruction.

Additionally, the play is an opportunity to explore intersectionality - how race interacts with other social categorizations such as class and power. While Othello holds military power and initially gains societal respect, his racial identity makes him vulnerable to manipulation and tragedy.

"Othello" thus offers a complex portrayal of race and otherness, which can initiate rich discussions about prejudice, identity, and belonging, topics that continue to define and challenge contemporary societies. The persistent resonance of these themes highlights the timeless relevance of Shakespeare's work and its ability to mirror and critique societal norms and issues.

Gender dynamics

"Othello" by William Shakespeare is a play that offers a valuable exploration of gender dynamics and misogyny, providing a critique that remains relevant in contemporary discourse. It explores societal expectations of women, their treatment, and the tragic consequences of unchecked misogyny.

Gender Roles and Expectations

Shakespeare presents a patriarchal Venetian society in which women are expected to be obedient and chaste. They are largely valued for their beauty and fidelity. Desdemona, in particular, epitomizes the societal expectations of women in her time. She is dutiful and gentle, and her attachment to Othello is defined by her loyalty and love.

However, she is also a character who displays a degree of independence and assertiveness, challenging the norms of her society. This is evidenced when she defends her love for Othello in front of her father Brabantio and the Venetian council in Act 1, Scene 3: "And so much duty as my mother showed / To you, preferring you before her father, / So much I challenge that I may profess / Due to the Moor my lord."

Misogyny and its Consequences

The play provides an in-depth exploration of the misogynistic attitudes of its time. Women are seen as possessions or objects. Iago refers to women dismissively, categorizing them as either obedient wives or adulteresses: "You rise to play and go to bed to work." (Act 2, Scene 1). Othello himself, driven by Iago's manipulation, starts to see Desdemona through a similar lens, viewing her imagined infidelity as a betrayal of his possession of her.

The unchecked misogyny in the play ultimately leads to tragic consequences. The false accusation of infidelity against Desdemona, primarily based on her supposed deviation from the societal norms of a dutiful and obedient woman, results in her death.

Contemporary Relevance

The issues of gender dynamics and misogyny are still prominent in contemporary society. While strides have been made towards gender equality, expectations of traditional gender roles persist in many cultures. Women continue to struggle for autonomy, often facing backlash when they challenge patriarchal norms.

The treatment of women as property or objects is a form of misogyny that, sadly, remains present today. The #MeToo movement, for example, arose as a response to systemic sexual harassment and assault, often stemming from a sense of entitlement towards women.

"Othello" allows readers to delve into these contemporary issues through its narrative, offering the chance to discuss and critique the damaging effects of such societal norms. Desdemona's death serves as a stark reminder of the dire consequences that can arise from unchecked misogyny and jealousy.

Moreover, the play provides a chance to discuss intersectionality and how race and gender interplay to heighten Othello and Desdemona's vulnerabilities. Othello, as a black man, is susceptible to Iago's manipulations due to societal prejudice. Desdemona, as a woman, is subject to restrictive norms and eventually becomes a victim of Othello's misguided rage.

In conclusion, "Othello" serves as a mirror reflecting societal attitudes towards gender and power, and the exploration of these themes within the text continues to hold significance in contemporary discourse. The portrayal of the tragic consequences of misogyny, jealousy, and societal expectations serve as a potent critique, lending the play a timeless relevance.

Manipulation and 'Fake News'

Shakespeare's "Othello" explores manipulation and deception, themes that are particularly relevant today given the prevalence of 'fake news' and misinformation. The character of Iago functions as a master manipulator, crafting untruths and half-truths to serve his malicious intent, much like the spreaders of 'fake news' in the contemporary digital age.

Iago and Manipulation

Iago's manipulation is central to the tragedy of "Othello." He is adept at exploiting the fears and insecurities of others to achieve his ends. His deception is multi-faceted: he pretends loyalty to Othello while secretly undermining him, and he manipulates Roderigo's love for Desdemona for his own financial gain.

A significant part of Iago's scheme is the use of misinformation. He plants the idea of Desdemona's infidelity in Othello's mind without providing any concrete evidence, knowing that the mere suggestion would prey on Othello's insecurities: "Look to your wife; observe her well with Cassio" (Act 3, Scene 3). Iago also manipulates the truth when he uses the handkerchief - a token of love between Desdemona and Othello - as false evidence of Desdemona's unfaithfulness.

'Fake News' and Contemporary Relevance

The dynamics of Iago's manipulation echo the contemporary issues surrounding 'fake news.' Today, misinformation is often used as a tool to manipulate public opinion, incite fear, or delegitimize truths. Much like Iago's use of untruths to exploit Othello's fears and insecurities, 'fake news' is often tailored to prey on the pre-existing beliefs, biases, or fears of its audience, making it a powerful tool for manipulation.

The concept of 'echo chambers' also finds resonance in the play. Once Othello starts to believe in Desdemona's infidelity, he becomes trapped in his own mind, only seeking information that confirms his suspicions, similar to how 'echo chambers' reinforce and amplify a specific viewpoint.

Iago's success lies in his ability to craft a narrative that is believable to his audience. Similarly, 'fake news' is often most effective when it contains elements of truth or when it confirms the existing biases of its recipients.

Effects and Consequences

The consequences of Iago's manipulation are disastrous, leading to mistrust, broken relationships, and deaths. This highlights the destructive power of misinformation, a warning that remains relevant today as societies grapple with the ramifications of 'fake news' - from strained interpersonal relationships to violence and social unrest.

The eventual unmasking of Iago's deceit is a reminder of the importance of truth and the necessity of critical thinking, especially in the age of digital information. However, the damage done is irreversible, suggesting that the fight against 'fake news' and manipulation must be preventative rather than reactionary.

In conclusion, the themes of manipulation and deception in "Othello" provide significant insight into the contemporary problem of 'fake news.' The play serves as a timeless exploration of the destructive power of misinformation, reinforcing the importance of truth, critical thinking, and media literacy in today's increasingly connected world.

— · —

Jealousy and toxic masculinity

In "Othello," William Shakespeare paints a vivid portrait of jealousy and toxic masculinity, which has contemporary resonance given the ongoing discussions surrounding gender norms and mental health. The tragic downfall of Othello stems from an uncontrolled jealousy and an internalization of toxic masculine norms, allowing for the exploration of these issues within a modern context.

Jealousy: The Green-Eyed Monster

At the heart of Othello's tragic downfall is his consuming jealousy. Iago cunningly manipulates him into believing that his wife, Desdemona, is unfaithful with his lieutenant, Cassio. Despite the lack of concrete evidence, Othello is overcome by this idea, which is largely driven by his own insecurities. He says, "O, beware, my lord, of jealousy! / It is the green-eyed monster, which doth mock / The meat it feeds on." (Act 3, Scene 3). This jealousy ultimately leads Othello to murder Desdemona.

Toxic Masculinity and its Effects

In the context of the play, Othello's jealousy is rooted in a sense of damaged masculinity and honor. He feels emasculated by the perceived infidelity, and his response - a violent assertion of control - exemplifies toxic masculinity. Toxic masculinity refers to a set of norms that emphasizes traits such as dominance, emotional repression, and aggression as inherently male.

This is seen in how Othello's language and behavior change over the course of the play. He moves from a calm, eloquent, and respected leader to a man driven by rage and jealousy. His decision to kill Desdemona, which he sees as a just response to her supposed unfaithfulness, reflects the dangerous consequences of toxic masculinity: "Yet she must die, else she'll betray more men." (Act 5, Scene 2).

Contemporary Relevance

The exploration of jealousy and toxic masculinity in "Othello" remains relevant today. Jealousy, especially when tied to romantic relationships, continues to be a source of personal and interpersonal conflict. In an era where social media can amplify feelings of inadequacy and insecurity, the destructive power of jealousy is an essential contemporary conversation.

Toxic masculinity, too, is a prevalent issue. Modern society is grappling with how restrictive gender norms contribute to issues such as mental health problems, gender-based violence, and the perpetuation of a culture that discourages emotional expression in men. The #MeToo movement has also highlighted the damaging effects of toxic masculinity, with a focus on its role in fostering harmful power dynamics and sexual misconduct.

In "Othello," the tragic outcomes for both the male and female characters underscore the harm caused by toxic masculinity. The narrative serves as a powerful critique, highlighting the need for healthier, more flexible understandings of masculinity.

Furthermore, there is a chance to discuss intersectionality in this context - the ways in which race and gender interact to shape experiences. As a black man in a predominantly white society, Othello's actions are heavily influenced by his perceived need to fit within accepted norms, contributing to his eventual downfall.

Conclusion

"Othello" thus provides a nuanced exploration of jealousy and toxic masculinity, offering insights into these issues that continue to hold relevance today. As contemporary society works towards dismantling harmful gender norms and promoting mental health, the play's tragedy underscores the importance of these conversations. The story of Othello serves as a cautionary tale about the devastating consequences of unchecked jealousy and the internalization of toxic masculinity.

POWER AND CORRUPTION

In "Othello," William Shakespeare masterfully unravels the complex relationship between power and corruption, illuminating the various ways that authority can be used for personal gain and deception. These themes continue to hold strong relevance to the contemporary world, where issues of power abuse, corruption, and manipulative leadership often arise in political and social contexts.

Power Dynamics in Othello

The intricate power dynamics in "Othello" are expressed through various relationships, including those between Othello and Iago, Othello and Desdemona, and Iago and Roderigo. Iago's manipulation of these relationships demonstrates how power can be used to deceive and corrupt.

Iago uses his position as Othello's trusted ensign to spread false rumors about Desdemona's infidelity. Despite having no concrete evidence, Iago is able to convince Othello of Desdemona's unfaithfulness because of his perceived honesty and loyalty. Iago even refers to himself as "an honest man" (Act 2, Scene 3), emphasizing his deception.

Corruption and Manipulation

Corruption is clearly embodied in Iago, who uses his knowledge of other characters' weaknesses to manipulate them. He exploits Roderigo's love for Desdemona, Cassio's low tolerance for alcohol, and most importantly, Othello's insecurities about his outsider status and his love for Desdemona.

His manipulation is ultimately aimed at achieving his own personal goals - power and revenge. The corruption in Iago's actions lies in his readiness to cause harm, sow discord, and even induce death, showing a complete disregard for morality in his quest for power.

Contemporary Relevance

Power and corruption remain vital themes in the contemporary world, especially in the realms of politics and leadership. News reports abound with stories of leaders using their positions for personal gain, often through manipulative and deceptive tactics similar to Iago's.

The play also reveals the vulnerability of those in power to misinformation and deceit, which finds resonance in the current era where 'fake news' can have a significant influence on public opinion and political outcomes.

Shakespeare's portrayal of Othello as a tragic figure who succumbs to Iago's manipulation also opens up conversations about the burdens of leadership. Othello's downfall, driven by his insecurities and the pressures of his position, serves as a reminder that power can also make one vulnerable to manipulation and self-destruction.

Conclusion

In "Othello," Shakespeare provides an enduring exploration of power and corruption. The manipulation and deceit of Iago demonstrate the potential for power to corrupt, leading to disastrous outcomes. This narrative continues to offer important insights into contemporary issues of leadership, manipulation, and the misuse of power.

Through the characters of Othello and Iago, Shakespeare's play continues to serve as a cautionary tale about the destructive potential of power when used manipulatively, and the susceptibility of those in power to deception and corruption. As such, "Othello" remains a poignant text that continues to provide a critical lens through which we can examine and discuss issues of power and corruption in the contemporary world.

— • —

SUMMARY OF THE PLAY

"Othello" by William Shakespeare is a classic tragedy that revolves around the themes of jealousy, betrayal, revenge, and racism. Its main character, Othello, succumbs to the manipulations of his ensign, Iago, leading to the death of his wife Desdemona, his loyal lieutenant Cassio's downfall, and eventually his own demise.

The play opens in the city of Venice, where the wealthy and foolish Roderigo is distressed to learn that Desdemona, the woman he loves, has eloped with Othello, a Moorish general in the Venetian army. Iago, Othello's ensign, harbors a deep resentment towards Othello for promoting Cassio over him and vows revenge. He uses Roderigo's unrequited love for Desdemona to fuel his plot, assuring him that he can help win her back.

When the action moves to Cyprus, where Othello is sent to defend against a Turkish invasion, Iago's machinations begin in earnest. He gets Cassio drunk, which leads to a brawl and Cassio's demotion. Iago then suggests to Cassio that he should appeal to Desdemona to convince Othello to reinstate him. This innocent advice becomes the foundation upon which Iago constructs his plot.

Iago subtly plants seeds of doubt about Desdemona's faithfulness in Othello's mind. He capitalizes on Othello's insecurities about his race, his age, and his outsider status in Venetian society. Iago's wife, Emilia, unknowingly facilitates his plan when she hands over a handkerchief, a gift from Othello to Desdemona. Iago uses it as proof of Desdemona's infidelity.

Othello, consumed by jealousy and rage, demands proof of Desdemona's unfaithfulness from Iago. He believes Iago's lies and accepts the planted handkerchief as irrefutable evidence. Blinded by his insecurities and manipulated by Iago's deceptive words, Othello resolves to kill Desdemona and orders Iago to kill Cassio.

In the final act, Othello murders Desdemona, smothering her in the bed where they have shared their love. Emilia arrives to announce that Roderigo has been killed while attempting to murder Cassio, but she finds Desdemona dying. Before her last breath, Desdemona exonerates her husband, claiming she has killed herself.

When Emilia realizes that her husband is behind the tragic events, she reveals his treachery. Iago kills her to silence her, but it is too late. Othello, now understanding Iago's manipulations, is overcome with grief and stabs Iago, who survives. Othello then kills himself, and the play ends with Cassio, now restored as lieutenant, in charge of punishing Iago.

"Othello" is a harrowing exploration of envy, deceit, and the tragic consequences of unchecked emotions. It's a tragic narrative that delves into the depths of human emotion and the destructive potential of manipulation. It examines the intricacies of love and betrayal, the devastating effects of jealousy, the insidious nature of manipulation, and the potent intersections of race and power.

Throughout the play, the audience bears witness to the dismantling of Othello - a noble and respected general whose downfall is not due to his own inherent weakness but is brought about by the devious machinations of his trusted ensign. At the same time, it presents a stinging critique of the societal norms and prejudices that enable such a fall.

This narrative is as tragic as it is thought-provoking, making "Othello" a timeless piece of literature that continues to be studied, performed, and appreciated more than four centuries after its creation. Through "Othello," Shakespeare presents an enduring exploration of the darker sides of human nature, serving as a powerful reminder of the disastrous consequences of jealousy, manipulation, and prejudice.

— · —

ACT I

Act 1 of Shakespeare's "Othello" sets the stage for the impending tragedy, introducing the main characters and their conflicts. The act is comprised of three scenes, each contributing significantly to the plot's progression.

Scene 1:

The play opens in Venice, at night, with a conversation between Roderigo, a wealthy Venetian who has been paying Iago to help him win the heart of the beautiful Desdemona, and Iago, Othello's ensign. Roderigo is upset to learn from Iago that Desdemona has secretly married Othello, a Moorish general in the service of Venice.

Iago confesses to Roderigo that he harbors a deep hatred for Othello because Othello has promoted Michael Cassio, whom Iago considers less capable, to the position of lieutenant over him. Iago justifies his manipulation of Roderigo by stating that he is using Roderigo's money to fund his own revenge against Othello. This scene reveals Iago's manipulative nature and his master plan to use others to enact his revenge.

Scene 2:

The next scene takes place on a street in Venice, where Othello, Iago, and attendants with torches enter. Iago tells Othello that Roderigo has been slandering him, but he downplays the extent of the insults, concealing the fact that he has provoked Roderigo.

Just as Brabantio, Desdemona's father, arrives with a group of followers to accuse Othello of bewitching his daughter, a messenger comes from the Duke of Venice summoning Othello to deal with a crisis in Cyprus. Brabantio decides to take his accusation to the Duke.

Scene 3:

The final scene of Act 1 takes place in a council chamber, where the Duke and Senators are discussing a Turkish attack on Cyprus. When Othello arrives, Brabantio accuses him of enchanting his daughter with spells and magic potions.

Othello eloquently defends himself, saying that he won Desdemona's heart by telling her his adventurous and harrowing life story, full of battles, disasters, and danger. Desdemona is brought to the chamber, and she corroborates Othello's explanation, stating that she loves him for the hardships he has undergone.

The Duke, moved by their testimony, dismisses Brabantio's accusations and gives his blessing to their marriage. He then sends Othello to Cyprus to defend against the Turks, and Desdemona insists on accompanying her husband.

Iago, left alone on stage at the end of the scene, reveals his plan to manipulate Othello's jealousy by making him believe that Desdemona and Cassio are having an affair.

Act 1 ends with a cliffhanger as the audience is left wondering how Iago's plot will unfold, setting the stage for the tragic events to follow. This act highlights the themes of racism, manipulation, and betrayal, which are essential to the narrative of "Othello". It introduces the central conflicts, establishes the stakes, and starts the character arcs that will lead to their inevitable tragedy.

— · —

ACT 2

"Othello" Act 2 further builds tension and anticipation, as the setting shifts from Venice to Cyprus, and the characters navigate the beginnings of Iago's nefarious scheme. This act contains three scenes.

Scene 1:

This scene opens in a seaport in Cyprus, with Montano, Cyprus's governor, and two gentlemen discussing the tempestuous weather that they fear has drowned the Turkish fleet threatening Cyprus. A third gentleman arrives to announce that the Turkish fleet indeed has been destroyed.

Cassio arrives, bringing news of Othello's safety but uncertainty about Desdemona's ship. Desdemona, Iago, and Emilia (Iago's wife) arrive, safe from the storm. Roderigo also arrives, still manipulated by Iago to believe he can win Desdemona's love.

Iago privately instigates Roderigo to provoke Cassio when the opportunity arises. When Othello arrives and celebrates the safety of his officers and wife, the scene ends on a hopeful note, providing a contrast to the tragedy that will soon unfold.

Scene 2:

A brief scene, it serves as a transitional piece. A herald reads a proclamation issued by Othello, declaring that the island of Cyprus will celebrate the destruction of the Turkish fleet. The festivities will include revelry in the streets, a night off for the soldiers, and a party at the castle.

Scene 3:

In the castle's great hall, Othello gives an eloquent speech, thanking his hosts in Cyprus and asking his men to celebrate but remain disciplined. He assigns Cassio to guard duty and departs with Desdemona.

Left with Roderigo, Iago puts his plan into action. He gets Cassio drunk and persuades Roderigo to provoke him. When Montano tries to intervene, he is injured by the drunk and belligerent Cassio. Iago sends Roderigo to raise an alarm in the town.

Othello arrives, furious about the disorder. When he learns about Cassio's actions, he strips him of his rank. Cassio is devastated by the loss of his reputation. Iago suggests that Cassio ask Desdemona to persuade Othello to reinstate him. Alone on stage, Iago gloats over the success of his scheme and plans the next phase of his plot.

By the end of Act 2, Iago has successfully planted the seeds of his destructive plot. With Cassio stripped of his rank and convinced to seek Desdemona's assistance, the stage is set for the further manipulation of Othello's perceptions and emotions. This act presents the perfect illustration of Iago's manipulative prowess and reveals the precariousness of the characters' circumstances as they fall into his trap.

— · —

ACT 3

Act 3 of "Othello" dramatically deepens Iago's manipulation and starts the tragic downfall of Othello. The act contains four pivotal scenes.

Scene 1:

A brief scene, it opens with Cassio imploring a musician to serenade Othello, hoping this might soften the general's anger. A clown, a servant of Othello, makes fun of the musician. Eventually, Cassio requests Emilia, Iago's wife and Desdemona's attendant, to arrange a private meeting for him with Desdemona.

Scene 2:

Another short transitional scene where Othello sends Iago to deliver some letters. Othello mentions that he will inspect parts of the fortifications built by the Cypriots.

Scene 3:

This is the crucial scene where Iago's manipulation takes root. Cassio speaks to Desdemona, pleading for her intervention in his favor. She willingly agrees, highlighting her pure, kind nature, and unknowingly advancing Iago's plot.

When Othello and Iago arrive, Cassio hastily departs, arousing Othello's curiosity. Iago, feigning reluctance, insinuates that Cassio's behavior was suspicious. Desdemona advocates for Cassio, but this only serves to further arouse Othello's suspicions.

Iago skillfully continues to suggest Cassio's guilt without making direct accusations, thereby inciting Othello's jealousy. He even uses Othello's love for Desdemona against him, suggesting that because she deceived her own father to marry Othello, she might deceive Othello too.

Desdemona drops a handkerchief, a gift from Othello, which Emilia picks up and gives to Iago, who plans to leave it in Cassio's lodging as further "proof" of an affair.

Scene 4:

Desdemona and Emilia discuss Othello's strange behavior, who seems distressed and even slapped Desdemona when she mentioned Cassio. Othello, questioning Desdemona about the missing handkerchief, grows more suspicious when she cannot present it.

Meanwhile, Cassio has found the handkerchief, and he gives it to his mistress, Bianca, oblivious of its significance. He asks her to copy its embroidery for him, unwittingly making her a part of Iago's scheme.

By the end of Act 3, Othello, in his growing jealousy and suspicion, is a far cry from the composed, dignified figure of the previous acts. Iago's manipulation has caused him to doubt Desdemona's fidelity, setting the stage for tragedy. The handkerchief, a symbol of Othello's love and Desdemona's fidelity, becomes a tool of deception in Iago's hands, highlighting the destructive power of miscommunication and misplaced trust.

— · —

ACT 4

Act 4 of "Othello" escalates the tragic trajectory of the play, with Othello's doubts transforming into irrational jealousy, and Desdemona's confusion turning into fear. The act has three intense scenes.

Scene 1:

The act opens with Iago "confirming" Cassio's affair with Desdemona to Othello. He fabricates a story of Cassio talking in his sleep about Desdemona. He also mentions the handkerchief, falsely claiming that he saw it in Cassio's hand.

The overwhelmed Othello has a seizure. As he recovers, Iago arranges for him to overhear, but not see, a conversation between Iago and Cassio. Iago cleverly manipulates the conversation to make it appear as if Cassio is bragging about his affair with Desdemona. In reality, Cassio is talking about Bianca, his lover, who enters displaying the handkerchief, further "confirming" Othello's suspicions.

Othello, now fully convinced of his wife's infidelity, is enraged and vows revenge. He and Iago plan the murder of Desdemona and Cassio.

Scene 2:

Othello interrogates Emilia about Desdemona's behavior, but Emilia insists Desdemona is innocent. Despite this, Othello confronts Desdemona, calling her a whore. Devastated and confused, Desdemona turns to Iago and Emilia for support.

Iago continues to play the innocent bystander, feigning shock and disbelief at Othello's accusations. Roderigo confronts Iago, feeling cheated, but Iago manages to convince him to kill Cassio, claiming that this will secure him Desdemona.

Scene 3:

In the final scene of this act, Desdemona prepares for bed, heartbroken and confused. Emilia helps her and, in one of the play's most poignant moments, they discuss the nature of women's fidelity and men's jealousy.

Desdemona, her innocence and love for Othello undimmed, prays and retires to bed, singing a melancholic song about a woman abandoned by her lover. She asks Emilia to lay her wedding sheets on the bed, symbolizing her faithfulness and the tragic misunderstanding that led to the current situation.

Act 4 presents the horrifying transformation of Othello under the influence of Iago's manipulations. Desdemona's innocence becomes her doom, and the impending tragedy is almost tangible as the act closes. It also highlights Iago's exceptional skill of manipulation as he plays each character against the other, his control over the narrative so complete that even the audience can feel its chilling effect.

ACT 5

Act 5 of "Othello" brings the tragic climax and resolution of the play, as the characters confront the disastrous consequences of deception, jealousy, and misplaced trust. It consists of two intense scenes.

Scene 1:

In the dim streets of Cyprus, Iago and Roderigo wait to ambush Cassio. When Cassio appears, Roderigo attacks him but is wounded instead. Iago, in the ensuing confusion, stabs Cassio in the leg and exits, leaving both men wounded on the street.

Passersby, including Lodovico and Gratiano (Venetian noblemen), discover Cassio and send for help. Iago reappears, pretending to be shocked by the events. He kills Roderigo to silence him and then falsely blames Bianca for Cassio's injuries, using her emotional reaction as proof of her guilt. Iago's manipulation and control of the narrative are masterfully depicted in this scene.

Scene 2:

In the bedchamber, Othello stands over the sleeping Desdemona, preparing to kill her. He kisses her one last time, waking her. He accuses her of infidelity, and despite her desperate pleas of innocence, he smothers her with a pillow.

Emilia enters, announcing that Roderigo is dead and Cassio is wounded. Upon seeing the dead Desdemona, she calls for help, revealing Othello as the murderer. Before she dies, Desdemona insists she is responsible for her own death.

Othello defends his actions, citing Desdemona's alleged infidelity and the handkerchief as proof. A horrified Emilia exposes Iago's manipulations. Iago enters, and when his treachery is revealed, he kills Emilia and attempts to escape, but is captured.

Othello, realizing his fatal error, tries to kill Iago, but only wounds him. Overwhelmed by regret and grief, Othello delivers a moving speech, reminding the bystanders of his past service to Venice and his deep love for Desdemona. He then stabs himself and dies, lying next to Desdemona.

The play concludes with the apprehension of Iago, the appointment of Cassio as the governor of Cyprus, and the resolution to carry the tragic news back to Venice.

Act 5 is a shocking denouement of the tragic consequences of Iago's manipulations. It portrays the tragic downfall of Othello, a respected military general, due to his insecurities and Iago's machinations. It also highlights the innocence of Desdemona and the devastation that jealousy, mistrust, and deception can wreak on individuals and relationships. The act serves as a stern reminder of the dangerous consequences of unchecked emotions and the destructive power of manipulation.

MAIN CHARACTERS

The main characters in "Othello" include:

1. Othello: As the titular character, Othello is central to the drama. He is a Moorish general in the Venetian army, respected for his military prowess and leadership. His outsider status, both as a foreigner and a black man in a predominantly white society, make him vulnerable to insecurities about his marriage to the Venetian Desdemona. These insecurities are exploited by Iago to tragic ends. Othello represents the destructive power of jealousy and the tragic consequences of misplaced trust.

2. Iago: Iago is the villain of the play, a manipulative and cunning ensign in Othello's army. He is driven by resentment towards Othello for promoting Cassio over him and harbors unfounded suspicions that Othello has slept with his wife, Emilia. Iago represents the embodiment of evil and the destructive power of manipulation and deception.

3. Desdemona: Desdemona is Othello's loyal and loving wife. Despite her innocence, she becomes the victim of Othello's unfounded jealousy, spurred by Iago's manipulations. She represents purity, love, and the tragic innocence that falls prey to Iago's evil designs.

4. Cassio: Cassio is Othello's lieutenant, whose promotion incites Iago's revenge. Iago uses him as a pawn in his plot to make Othello believe that Desdemona is unfaithful. Cassio's reputation and relationship with Desdemona are exploited by Iago to advance his deceitful plot.

5. Emilia: Emilia is Iago's wife and Desdemona's attendant. Her role is pivotal as she unknowingly aids Iago's plot by giving him Desdemona's handkerchief, which he uses as false evidence of Desdemona's infidelity. In the end, she reveals Iago's manipulations, acting as a voice of truth and justice.

Each of these characters plays a critical role in the unfolding of the plot and in the exploration of the play's key themes. They all contribute to the dramatic impact of the play, the development of its tragic narrative, and its exploration of complex issues like race, trust, jealousy, love, manipulation, and power.

DESCRIBE OTHELLO

Othello, the protagonist of William Shakespeare's play of the same name, is one of the most complex characters in the Bard's oeuvre. A Moorish general serving in the Venetian army, Othello's military prowess, dignity, and articulate speech set him apart from his contemporaries, and yet his race and cultural background also mark him as an outsider, feeding his personal insecurities and vulnerability to manipulation.

From the outset of the play, Othello is depicted as a man of authority and honor. In Act 1, Scene 2, despite Iago's attempts to incite him into confrontation with Brabantio, Othello maintains his composure, stating, "Keep up your bright swords, for the dew will rust them" (1.2.59). He's able to rise above the xenophobia and racism he faces, securing his position in Venetian society through his heroic military service and his articulate speech.

Nevertheless, Othello's heroic qualities are coupled with a pronounced vulnerability. His love for Desdemona is passionate but also possessive, revealing his fear of losing her. When Iago starts insinuating Desdemona's infidelity, Othello is immediately thrown into doubt and suspicion. The ease with which he succumbs to Iago's manipulations can be attributed to his deep-seated insecurities about his outsider status and Desdemona's loyalty.

The imagery Othello uses to express his turmoil adds to the understanding of his character. As he contemplates Desdemona's alleged infidelity, he says, "O, it comes o'er my memory / As doth the raven o'er the infectious house, / Boding to all" (1.2.61-63). This metaphor reflects his darkening perspective and his deep despair.

Othello's downfall is tragically rapid. Once the seed of doubt is planted, his speech becomes fragmented and feverish, mirroring his crumbling sanity. His noble demeanor gives way to aggressive outbursts, such as when he strikes Desdemona in public (Act 4, Scene 1). Othello's tragic flaw – his jealousy and his readiness to believe the worst about his wife without substantial proof – leads him to murder the woman he loves, a stark contrast to the honorable general introduced at the play's beginning.

In Act 5, Scene 2, before he kills himself, Othello delivers a heart-rending soliloquy, urging the Venetians to speak of him as he is: "one that loved not wisely but too well; / Of one not easily jealous, but being wrought, / Perplexed in the extreme" (5.2.343-345). This self-evaluation underscores the tragedy of his character - a man who had potential for greatness but was undone by his insecurities and Iago's manipulations.

In conclusion, Othello is a tragically heroic figure whose personal insecurities lead him down a path of self-destruction. Despite his high status and the respect he commands, his perception of himself as an outsider, his propensity for jealousy, and his naivety make him susceptible to manipulation, ultimately leading to his tragic downfall. His journey from a dignified general to a murderous, jealous husband explores the human capacity for irrationality and self-destruction, making him one of Shakespeare's most poignant tragic heroes.

— · —

Describe Iago

Iago, the villain in William Shakespeare's "Othello," is often regarded as one of the most sinister characters in all of literature. His cunning, manipulative nature, his facility for deceit, and his seemingly motiveless malignancy make him a complex and deeply unsettling figure.

From the start, Iago's resentment of Othello is clear. He feels slighted by Othello's decision to promote the less experienced Cassio over him. As he reveals in his soliloquy in Act 1, Scene 3: "I know my price, I am worth no worse a place." He also nurtures a baseless suspicion that Othello has slept with his wife, Emilia, fueling his vindictive impulse.

However, these reasons seem insufficient to justify the depth of his malevolence, leading many to speculate that Iago represents a personification of pure evil. His primary motivation seems to be an innate and sadistic pleasure in creating chaos and suffering.

Iago's power lies in his ability to manipulate others by exploiting their weaknesses. He incites Brabantio's racist prejudices to turn him against Othello, uses Roderigo's love for Desdemona for his own gains, and, most destructively, preys on Othello's insecurities about his race and his marriage to Desdemona. His manipulation is so subtle that he maintains his appearance as an honest and loyal ensign, all the while plotting their downfall.

His language is a critical tool in his deception. He often speaks in innuendos, as when he subtly implants the idea of Desdemona's infidelity in Othello's mind in Act 3, Scene 3, suggesting, "I speak not yet of proof.

Look to your wife; observe her well with Cassio." His cunning use of language allows him to make others believe that his insinuations are their own conclusions.

Iago also breaks the fourth wall frequently, delivering soliloquies that reveal his true intentions to the audience. One of his most chilling lines is, "I am not what I am" (1.1.65), a confession of his duplicity that reflects his joy in deceit and manipulation. He showcases his nihilistic worldview in Act 2, Scene 3 when he states, "Virtue? A fig! 'Tis in ourselves that we are thus, or thus."

Ironically, Iago is honest only with the audience, making his character an even more compelling and unsettling presence. In his interactions with others, he feigns honesty and loyalty, but in his soliloquies, he delights in his deviousness, embodying the duplicitous nature of his character.

As the plot unfolds, Iago's manipulations become increasingly destructive. His machinations lead to the deaths of Othello, Desdemona, and Emilia, and the downfall of Cassio, ultimately revealing the depths of his depravity.

In conclusion, Iago is a character of profound complexity and disturbing amorality. His manipulation, deceit, and apparent lack of motive make him a chilling antagonist and a compelling study of villainy. His character serves as a reminder of the destructive potential of manipulation and unchecked ambition, making him one of the most memorable villains in literature.

— • —

DESCRIBE DESDEMONA

Desdemona, the heroine of William Shakespeare's "Othello," is a character of purity, love, and tragic innocence. Her journey from a loving wife to a victim of unfounded jealousy gives her character a heartbreaking pathos.

From the outset, Desdemona defies societal norms, marrying Othello, a Moor, for love despite his racial and cultural differences from her Venetian background. Her initial entrance in Act 1, Scene 3, gives us a glimpse of her eloquence, strength, and assertiveness. She openly confesses her love for Othello in front of her father, Brabantio, and the Venetian council, stating, "I saw Othello's visage in his mind, And to his honors and his valiant parts Did I my soul and fortunes consecrate" (1.3.248-250). She values Othello's character and bravery, suggesting that her love is profound and transcends superficial considerations.

Desdemona is often portrayed as an ideal of womanhood—virtuous, beautiful, and obedient. However, her character holds more complexities. Her love for Othello is not just a passive acceptance but an active choice, showing a boldness that is rare for women of her time. Her decision to elope with Othello exhibits her strength, independent spirit, and non-conformity.

Despite her nobility and loyalty, Desdemona becomes a tragic victim due to her naivety and unwavering faith in Othello. She is completely oblivious to the suspicions Othello harbors about her, even when she is on the verge of death. Her innocence in the face of Othello's escalating jealousy is particularly poignant. In Act 4, Scene 2, even after being struck and publicly humiliated by Othello, she weeps for him, illustrating her boundless empathy and love.

Her relationship with Emilia, her maid, gives us more insights into her character. Desdemona's lack of worldly experience contrasts sharply with Emilia's cynical views on men and marriage. In Act 4, Scene 3, Desdemona adamantly asserts she would not be unfaithful to Othello for "the whole world" even when Emilia suggests women have the same desires as men.

Her tragic end, smothered by Othello in her marriage bed, is one of the most haunting scenes in the play. Even in her dying breath in Act 5, Scene 2, she shows her love and loyalty towards Othello by lying about her death, stating, "Nobody—I myself. Farewell. Commend me to my kind lord." These are some of her last words, a poignant testament to her character.

Ultimately, Desdemona's character reflects the destructive consequences of jealousy and unfounded suspicions. Her downfall is not due to any personal flaws but rather her inability to defend herself against the machinations of Iago and the jealousy of Othello. She embodies the tragic innocence that falls prey to the destructive designs of jealousy and manipulations.

Desdemona remains one of Shakespeare's most significant female characters. Her unwavering love, loyalty, assertiveness, and tragic innocence make her a compelling character. However, her downfall serves as a harsh critique of societal norms and prejudices and a reminder of the tragic consequences of unfounded jealousy and suspicion.

DESCRIBE CASSIO

Michael Cassio, a central character in Shakespeare's "Othello," is depicted as a handsome, courteous, and capable young man. His role is pivotal in the tragedy that unfolds due to his unwitting involvement in Iago's malevolent plot.

Cassio is Othello's loyal lieutenant, chosen for the position over Iago, thereby igniting the latter's resentment and setting the stage for the tragic events that follow. His military skill is highly esteemed by Othello, who praises him, saying, "a Florentine,/ A fellow almost damn'd in a fair wife;/ That never set a squadron in the field,/ Nor the division of a battle knows" (1.1.21-24). Cassio's reputation for military competence is thus established early on in the play.

However, Cassio is more than just a capable soldier. He is a man of good manners and high learning, qualities that further endear him to Othello but also make him susceptible to Iago's schemes. His polished manners and sophisticated rhetoric stand in sharp contrast to Iago's more blunt and deceptive speech.

Cassio's major flaw, which Iago exploits, is his inability to hold his liquor. In Act 2, Scene 3, Iago induces Cassio into drinking excessively, causing him to lose control and fight with Roderigo and Montano. As a result, Cassio is demoted, setting Iago's scheme into motion. Cassio laments his actions, regretting that he has lost his reputation, which he calls "the immortal part of myself...my occupation" (2.3.261-264).

Cassio also develops a close relationship with Desdemona as he seeks her help to regain his position. His courteous demeanor towards Desdemona is misconstrued as a romantic interest by the increasingly jealous Othello. In Act 3, Scene 3, Cassio's comment on Desdemona, "She holds it a vice in her goodness not to do more than she is requested" (3.3.12-14), shows his respect and admiration for her. However, his interactions with Desdemona feed Othello's growing suspicion, another element of Iago's manipulative plot.

Despite being a pawn in Iago's game, Cassio is the only major character who survives the tragedy. However, he does so bearing the weight of the loss of his friends and the knowledge of his role, albeit unwitting, in their downfall. Cassio's closing lines, "This did I fear, but thought he had no weapon; For he was great of heart," (5.2.358-359) reflect his deep sorrow at Othello's death and his profound regret for the tragic events.

Cassio's character serves as a foil to both Othello and Iago. His courteous manners and genuine respect for Desdemona contrast sharply with Othello's irrational jealousy and Iago's disrespect towards women. His naïvety and trust make him an easy target for Iago's manipulations, contrasting Iago's cunning nature.

In conclusion, Cassio is a character that embodies the tragedy of being caught in the web of others' deceptions. He is an emblem of the innocent lives that can be destroyed due to the machinations of others. His character offers a crucial perspective on the themes of trust, manipulation, and reputation in the play.

— · —

DESCRIBE EMILIA

Emilia, one of the main characters in Shakespeare's "Othello", is Iago's wife and Desdemona's attendant. Her character is complex, with an evolution that shows her moving from a somewhat passive participant in Iago's plots to a moral beacon and truth-teller by the play's end.

Emilia begins the play largely in the background. She is aware of her husband Iago's deep resentment of Othello but seems unaware of the full extent of his malevolence. She unwittingly assists in Iago's plans when, in Act 3, Scene 3, she hands over Desdemona's handkerchief, a token Othello gave to his wife as a symbol of their love. Iago uses this handkerchief to fuel Othello's jealousy, leading to Desdemona's tragic end.

While initially complicit in Iago's scheme, Emilia's character begins to evolve as the plot progresses. She offers a sharp critique of societal expectations for women and their treatment by men. In Act 4, Scene 3, during a conversation with Desdemona, Emilia articulates her pragmatic view of marriage and infidelity, saying, "But I do think it is their husbands' faults / If wives do fall" (4.3.89-90), a stark contrast to Desdemona's innocent and steadfast loyalty.

Despite her practical views on marriage, Emilia is loyal to Desdemona and consistently expresses her love and concern for her. It's this loyalty that starts to turn her against Iago. She observes his behavior and Othello's growing mistrust and jealousy, causing her to question her understanding of the men around her.

In the play's tragic climax, Emilia emerges as a heroine. Upon discovering that Othello has murdered Desdemona based on false infidelity accusations, she fearlessly confronts him in Act 5, Scene 2, boldly stating, "O thou dull Moor! That handkerchief thou speak'st of / I found by fortune and did give my husband" (5.2.226-227). Even when threatened by Othello and begged by Iago to be silent, Emilia stands firm and uncovers her husband's heinous manipulation, leading to Iago's arrest and her own death.

Emilia's character provides a counterpoint to Desdemona's. While Desdemona is portrayed as a paragon of purity and innocence, Emilia is more worldly, cynical, and outspoken about the injustices women face. Her powerful monologue about the double standards and unfair expectations imposed on women remains a compelling critique of gender relations.

At the same time, Emilia's moral awakening and her courageous decision to unveil the truth form a significant turning point in the play. Her actions, though leading to her death, restore the moral order that Iago's actions had shattered.

In conclusion, Emilia's character in "Othello" offers a nuanced exploration of womanhood, loyalty, and morality. While she begins the play complicit in her husband's plotting, she ultimately becomes a voice of truth and moral authority, proving instrumental in revealing Iago's treachery. Her transformation is a testament to her integrity and love for Desdemona, offering a stark contrast to the malicious manipulations of her husband.

— · —

MINOR CHARACTERS

There are several minor characters in "Othello" whose contributions to the plot and themes are significant, even though they may not appear on stage as often as the major characters. Here are a few of them:

1. **Roderigo**: Roderigo is a Venetian gentleman who is in love with Desdemona and thus easily manipulated by Iago. Iago uses Roderigo's infatuation with Desdemona to further his plot against Othello, promising that he can help Roderigo win Desdemona's affection. Roderigo is a somewhat comic figure, but his role is crucial in forwarding the plot, as his willingness to do anything to win Desdemona makes him a useful pawn in Iago's schemes. His murder at Iago's hands in the final act (5.1) brings Iago's duplicity and treachery to the fore.

2. **Brabantio**: Brabantio is Desdemona's father, a senator in Venice. He is important in establishing the societal background against which the action takes place. He's outraged when he learns of Desdemona's elopement with Othello, exclaiming "O thou foul thief, where hast thou stowed my daughter?" (1.2.62). This reaction helps set up the racial and social prejudices that come into play throughout the narrative. He also foreshadows Othello's downfall when he warns Othello, "She has deceived her father, and may thee" (1.3.292), planting the first seeds of doubt about Desdemona's faithfulness.

3. **Bianca**: Bianca is a courtesan in Cyprus and Cassio's lover. Despite her minor role, Bianca's presence serves a critical function in Iago's plot. When Cassio gives her the handkerchief that Iago had planted on him, Bianca unknowingly becomes part of the manipulation that convinces Othello of Desdemona's unfaithfulness. Her love for Cassio also mirrors the main plot's tragic love story, showing the effects of jealousy and suspicion in relationships.

4. **Duke of Venice**: The Duke is the authoritative figure in Venice who respects Othello and entrusts him with the defense of Cyprus against the Turks. His respect for Othello, despite Brabantio's racist accusations in Act 1, Scene 3, showcases the high regard in which Othello is held in Venetian society, making his eventual downfall even more tragic.

5. **Montano**: As the former governor of Cyprus, Montano's main role is in Act 2, Scene 3, where his injury in the brawl with a drunken Cassio gives Othello a reason to demote Cassio, thereby advancing Iago's plot. Montano's respect for Othello also highlights Othello's honorable reputation before his downfall.

Each of these minor characters contributes to the advancement of the plot, the development of the major characters, or the illumination of the play's major themes, such as jealousy, manipulation, and the tragic consequences of deceit.

— • —

IMPORTANT RELATIONSHIPS

"Othello" is a play that explores complex human relationships in a society rife with prejudice and deceit. Below are several key relationships that drive the play's action and illuminate its themes:

Othello and Desdemona: This central relationship is the heart of the play. Their marriage is unconventional due to differences in their race, age, and social status. Their love for each other appears genuine and passionate, as seen in Act 1, Scene 3, when Desdemona tells her father and the Venetian senators, "I saw Othello's visage in his mind, And to his honors and his valiant parts Did I my soul and fortunes consecrate" (1.3.247-249). Despite their love, their relationship is marred by societal pressures and Iago's machinations.

Othello's insecurity about fitting into Venetian society, his self-doubt, and the fear of losing Desdemona makes him susceptible to Iago's insinuations of Desdemona's infidelity. It's these insecurities that lead to the ultimate tragic end of their relationship. Othello's murder of Desdemona in Act 5 Scene 2 is a horrifying climax of the play, demonstrating how jealousy and suspicion can destroy even the deepest love.

Othello and Iago: Iago's relationship with Othello is one of the most destructive in the play. Iago is Othello's ensign, a position that places him in close proximity to Othello but not as close as he'd like to be – he is embittered that Cassio was promoted to lieutenant instead of him. This fuels his resentment of Othello, causing him to craft an intricate plot of revenge.

Their relationship is fraught with manipulation and deceit. Iago exploits Othello's trust in him and manipulates his insecurities and fears. Othello, on the other hand, sees Iago as "honest Iago" and often refers to him as such, falling into his trap. This relationship's destructive nature culminates in the tragic deaths of Desdemona, Emilia, Roderigo, and Othello himself.

Desdemona and Emilia: The relationship between Desdemona and Emilia, her attendant and Iago's wife, provides a contrast to the relationships between men in the play. Desdemona and Emilia's friendship is marked by honesty and mutual respect. In Act 4, Scene 3, they share a candid conversation about love and infidelity, showcasing their differing perspectives on these topics.

Emilia's loyalty to Desdemona surpasses her loyalty to her husband. When she realizes Iago's role in manipulating Othello against Desdemona, she chooses to reveal his deceit, knowing that it might cost her life. Emilia's defense of Desdemona's virtue to Othello, even at the cost of her own life, marks one of the most powerful moments in the play.

Iago and Emilia: This relationship contrasts sharply with Othello and Desdemona's relationship. Iago and Emilia's marriage is depicted as loveless, filled with mistrust and manipulation. Iago often belittles Emilia, and Emilia, in return, has a cynical view of her husband. Despite this, Emilia is unwittingly drawn into Iago's plot against Othello when she hands over Desdemona's handkerchief. The climax of their relationship occurs when Emilia realizes Iago's treachery and reveals it, resulting in Iago killing her.

Iago and Roderigo: Roderigo's infatuation with Desdemona makes him an easy target for Iago's manipulation. Iago uses him to set his plans in motion, while Roderigo naively believes that Iago is helping him win Desdemona. This relationship underscores the theme of manipulation and deception, showing how Iago is able to use others for his own ends.

In conclusion, the relationships in "Othello" are instrumental in driving the play's plot and illuminating its themes. Each relationship, whether marked by love, trust, manipulation, or betrayal, helps create a narrative filled with tension and tragedy. The complex dynamics within these relationships serve to explore human nature's dark side, providing a timeless critique of how jealousy, mistrust, and manipulation can lead to devastating consequences.

OTHELLO AND DESDEMONA'S RELATIONSHIP

Othello and Desdemona's relationship forms the dramatic core of Shakespeare's "Othello." Their bond, steeped in passionate love, cultural differences, and tragic misunderstanding, is one of the most complex and tragically fated in all of Shakespeare's plays.

From the start, Othello and Desdemona's relationship is presented as unconventional and scandalous due to the differences in their racial and social backgrounds. Othello is a Moor and a distinguished military general, while Desdemona is a young, white, and high-born Venetian woman. When they elope, it's against societal norms, provoking shock and disapproval in Venice, particularly from Desdemona's father, Brabantio, who accuses Othello of bewitching his daughter (Act 1, Scene 3). Despite this, their love is portrayed as deep and sincere. Othello wins Desdemona's love with his heroic tales of his adventurous life, and Desdemona defies societal expectations to marry the man she genuinely loves.

However, their relationship is tested when they move to Cyprus, away from the familiar Venetian society. Here, Iago's machinations begin to unravel their bond. Othello's trust in Desdemona is the cornerstone of their relationship, yet it is this trust that Iago systematically dismantles. When Iago begins to plant seeds of doubt in Othello's mind about Desdemona's fidelity, it isn't merely her honesty that is questioned but the very foundation of their relationship.

Othello's insecurities about his race and age and his outsider status in Venetian society make him particularly vulnerable to Iago's manipulations. His outsider status becomes a tool in Iago's hands, enabling him to convince Othello that Desdemona could be unfaithful. Despite Desdemona's constant assertions of her love and loyalty, Othello's faith in her is shattered. This insecurity is embodied in Othello's statement in Act 3, Scene 3: "Haply, for I am black... She's gone. I am abused, and my relief must be to loathe her."

As the play progresses, Othello's suspicion turns into destructive jealousy, leading him to demand "ocular proof" of Desdemona's unfaithfulness (Act 3, Scene 3). Othello's eventual acceptance of Iago's fabricated evidence (the handkerchief) shows the extent of his transformation from a loving husband to a jealous murderer.

Desdemona, in contrast, remains steadfast in her love for Othello, even in the face of his growing hostility. Even at the moment of her death, she maintains her loyalty to Othello, claiming she herself is responsible for her death, telling Emilia, "A guiltless death I die" (Act 5, Scene 2). This tragically illuminates her innocence and unwavering love.

In conclusion, the relationship between Othello and Desdemona is a tragic study of how societal pressures, personal insecurities, and calculated manipulation can corrupt the purest love. Their relationship, which begins as a union of two loving souls, is systematically poisoned until it culminates in a heartbreaking tragedy. Their story serves as a timeless reminder of the destructive power of jealousy and the tragic consequences of mistrust.

— · —

OTHELLO AND IAGO'S RELATIONSHIP

The relationship between Othello and Iago forms one of the critical axes around which "Othello" revolves. It is a complex relationship shaped by social status, resentment, trust, and manipulation, and its evolution ultimately drives the tragic events of the play.

At the start of the play, Othello and Iago are military colleagues. Othello, as the General, holds the superior rank, while Iago is his ensign. Othello's decision to promote Cassio to lieutenant over Iago, revealed in Act 1 Scene 1, establishes a crucial rift in their relationship. Iago feels betrayed and humiliated, believing himself more deserving of the position. This perceived slight is the catalyst for Iago's personal vendetta against Othello.

Iago's resentment is further amplified by a rumour that Othello has slept with his wife, Emilia. While this rumour is never confirmed, it adds a layer of personal bitterness to Iago's professional jealousy. Iago's enmity towards Othello is explicitly stated in Act 1 Scene 3 when he says, "I hate the Moor."

In contrast, Othello sees Iago as a trusted and honest confidante. Othello often refers to Iago as "honest Iago," an ironic twist given Iago's duplicity. This trust is a crucial element of their relationship and a key factor in Iago's ability to manipulate Othello. Othello's faith in Iago allows the latter to plant seeds of doubt about Desdemona's fidelity subtly.

As the play progresses, Iago uses Othello's trust in him to orchestrate a series of events that would make Othello suspicious of Desdemona's loyalty. By exploiting Othello's insecurities about his race, age, and outsider status, Iago manipulates him into believing that his wife, Desdemona, has been unfaithful with Cassio.

Iago's manipulative skills are evident in Act 3 Scene 3, when he plants the idea of Desdemona's infidelity in Othello's mind, carefully constructing a web of deception that eventually drives Othello to murder. Iago's words, "O, beware, my lord, of jealousy; It is the green-ey'd monster, which doth mock The meat it feeds on" (3.3.165-167), provoke Othello's transformation from a loving husband to a jealous murderer.

The climax of their relationship is reached in Act 5 Scene 2, where Iago's deceit is finally revealed, and Othello realizes that he has been manipulated into murdering his innocent wife. At this point, Othello's trust in Iago transforms into utter loathing, leading Othello to attack Iago, marking the tragic outcome of their relationship.

In conclusion, Othello and Iago's relationship serves as a narrative vehicle for exploring themes of trust, manipulation, jealousy, and revenge. Iago's manipulation of Othello's trust and the tragic consequences that follow expose the devastating potential of deceit and the frailty of trust. Their relationship illustrates how a single person's malevolent intent can destroy the lives of many, turning love into hatred and trust into suspicion. This relationship serves as a timeless reminder of the catastrophic results that deception and mistrust can bring about in human relationships.

DESDEMONA AND EMILIA'S RELATIONSHIP

Desdemona and Emilia's relationship in "Othello" is both central and subversive to the play's themes of gender, power, and loyalty. This relationship gives voice to the experiences of women in a male-dominated society, revealing the complexities of womanhood and friendship in the Elizabethan era and beyond.

Desdemona and Emilia, despite their differing social statuses – Desdemona as the aristocratic wife of the General, Othello, and Emilia as a middle-class woman married to Iago, Othello's ensign – share a bond that transcends these societal constructs. Emilia serves as Desdemona's lady-in-waiting, a relationship that combines aspects of servitude and companionship.

Their dynamic is first depicted as somewhat conventional of the time. Emilia, in her role as lady-in-waiting, is expected to be loyal to Desdemona, and she carries out her duties faithfully. However, as the play unfolds, their relationship evolves into a deeper and more complex friendship, one which provides insight into their shared experiences as women in a patriarchal society.

Emilia's practical and often cynical view of men and marriage serves as a stark contrast to Desdemona's idealistic and romantic notions. For instance, in Act 3, Scene 4, Emilia suggests that men are universally unfaithful, challenging Desdemona's idealistic view of Othello. Despite their contrasting views, their relationship is based on mutual respect and empathy.

This is most clearly evidenced in Act 4, Scene 3, the famous "Willow Scene," in which the women converse on matters of love, marriage, and fidelity. Here, the complexity and intimacy of their friendship are most palpable. Emilia's speech about the double standards for men and women in matters of fidelity sheds light on her own marriage and the general treatment of women in their society.

However, their relationship becomes strained due to Emilia's unknowing complicity in Iago's scheme. Emilia takes the handkerchief (which Othello had given to Desdemona as a love token) and gives it to Iago, not realizing he will use it as "evidence" of Desdemona's supposed infidelity.

The tragedy of Desdemona's death leads to the final transformation of their relationship. Emilia fiercely defends Desdemona's innocence, leading to her confrontation with Iago and her ultimate death. Here, Emilia's loyalty to Desdemona overrides her loyalty to her husband, showcasing her deep bond with Desdemona and her moral courage.

In conclusion, Desdemona and Emilia's relationship provides a nuanced portrayal of female friendship in a patriarchal context. Their interactions offer a critique of the gender dynamics of their time, as they navigate their roles as wives within the constraints of their society. Through their shared experiences, they expose the oppressive social conditions women face, while their friendship provides a source of support and understanding. Their tragic end emphasizes the cost of their society's patriarchal norms and underscores the tragic consequences of deception and manipulation.

IAGO AND EMILIA'S RELATIONSHIP

Iago and Emilia's relationship in "Othello" provides a stark contrast to the titular couple's. Their relationship is fraught with power struggles, manipulation, and a profound lack of understanding, each aspect reinforcing the play's overarching themes of deception, power, and gender dynamics.

At the play's outset, the audience perceives a clear power dynamic with Iago, Emilia's husband, occupying the dominant role. This male dominance was typical in Elizabethan society. Iago is dismissive and disrespectful towards Emilia, often belittling her intelligence and speaking crudely about women in general. For instance, in Act 2, Scene 1, Iago crudely asserts, "You rise to play and go to bed to work," a demeaning perspective on women's roles.

Emilia, on the other hand, is caught in a paradox. She is both a dutiful wife, eager to please her husband and a woman with a sharp mind who understands the unfairness of the patriarchal society in which she lives. She often openly disagrees with Iago's cynical and misogynistic views about women and marriage, demonstrating her wit and perceptive insight into the inequities of their society.

Their relationship reaches a turning point when Emilia, unwittingly, becomes instrumental in Iago's devious plot against Othello. She gives Iago Desdemona's handkerchief, not knowing that Iago will use it as "proof" of Desdemona's unfaithfulness. Here, the audience witnesses a clear example of Iago's manipulative nature, exploiting his wife's trust for his malevolent plans.

Emilia's revelation of her husband's true character towards the end of the play offers a dramatic climax to their relationship. Upon discovering that Iago has manipulated events to cause Desdemona's death, Emilia chooses loyalty to her mistress over her husband. In Act 5, Scene 2, Emilia exclaims, "I will not charm my tongue; I am bound to speak," refusing to stay silent about Iago's treachery despite the danger she faces.

This final act of defiance from Emilia underlines her character development and the evolution of her relationship with Iago. It reflects her recognition of the destructive influence of Iago's deceit and her courage to defy her husband, revealing the truth at the cost of her own life.

In conclusion, Iago and Emilia's relationship serves as a key exploration of power dynamics, manipulation, and the treatment of women in a patriarchal society. Their marriage contrasts sharply with the love between Othello and Desdemona, portraying a darker side of relationships marked by disrespect, exploitation, and deceit. The transformation in their relationship from apparent marital normalcy to the revelation of manipulative deceit provides a poignant commentary on the destructive power of dishonesty and the courage it takes to reveal the truth.

Iago and Roderigo's relationship

Iago and Roderigo's relationship in "Othello" can be described as a masterclass in manipulation. Iago, a Machiavellian character par excellence, effectively uses Roderigo's vulnerabilities and desires to achieve his own malicious ends. This relationship serves as a critical device to set the plot in motion, while also reinforcing the themes of manipulation, deception, and self-interest.

Roderigo, a Venetian gentleman infatuated with Desdemona, serves as a perfect pawn in Iago's hands. From the beginning of the play, it's clear that Roderigo is a victim of Iago's cunning, evident in Iago's manipulation of Roderigo's unrequited love for Desdemona. Iago promises to help Roderigo win Desdemona, while in fact, he plans to use him as a means to wreak havoc and revenge on Othello.

Iago's manipulation of Roderigo is evident in his cunning use of language and rhetoric. He expertly stokes Roderigo's jealousy and fear, convincing him that Desdemona's love for Othello is merely a fleeting infatuation. In Act 1, Scene 3, Iago tells Roderigo, "If she had been blessed, she would never have loved the Moor," exploiting Roderigo's racial prejudices and inflaming his hopes.

Throughout the play, Roderigo is led to act on Iago's advice, leading him to financial ruin and, eventually, his death. Roderigo becomes an accomplice in Iago's scheme against Cassio and Othello, demonstrating how easily manipulated he is. Despite Roderigo's occasional doubts about Iago's honesty, such as in Act 4, Scene 2, where he says, "I do not find that thou dealest justly with me," Iago always manages to convince him otherwise, exhibiting Iago's skill as a manipulator.

Their relationship is ultimately defined by Iago's manipulation and Roderigo's blind trust. This dynamic reaches its climax in Act 5, Scene 1, where Iago convinces Roderigo to attack Cassio. When the plan backfires, Iago does not hesitate to kill Roderigo to cover his tracks, thus signifying the utter lack of genuine regard or loyalty in their relationship.

In summary, Iago and Roderigo's relationship provides a disturbing exploration of manipulation and self-serving deceit. Their relationship highlights Iago's manipulative abilities and the tragic consequences of such deception. Iago uses Roderigo's blind love for Desdemona to drive the play's tragic events, ultimately leading to Roderigo's demise. This relationship is a stark reminder of the destructive power of manipulation and the tragic fate of those who fall prey to it.

— • —

Conflicts

In William Shakespeare's "Othello," various forms of conflict shape the narrative, driving the action and influencing character dynamics. The conflicts stem from personal ambitions, love and jealousy, racial and cultural differences, and manipulative deceit, all of which culminate in the play's tragic ending.

At the core of the play is the personal conflict of Iago, a character motivated by jealousy and a desire for revenge. He is incensed by Othello's decision to promote Cassio over him. This personal slight becomes the genesis of Iago's intricate plot against Othello. His resentment manifests in Act 1, Scene 1 when he says, "I know my price, I am worth no worse a place," emphasizing his perceived injustice.

This initial conflict spirals into a more complex one involving love and jealousy. Iago manipulates Othello into believing that his wife Desdemona is unfaithful. Iago's insinuations about Desdemona's alleged infidelity with Cassio induce a deep-seated jealousy in Othello, leading to a devastating internal conflict. This is evident in Act 3, Scene 3, where Othello expresses his turmoil, stating, "Why did I marry?... O curse of marriage!"

Another conflict that profoundly influences the play is the racial and cultural tension that stems from Othello's status as an outsider. As a Moor in a predominantly white Venetian society, Othello faces racism and prejudice. This cultural conflict is exploited by Iago, who uses racial slurs and stereotypes to belittle Othello and further his schemes. Racial prejudice is also evident in Brabantio's outrage at Desdemona's marriage to Othello in Act 1, Scene 2, where he accuses Othello of witchcraft, suggesting that a white woman could only fall for a black man under unnatural circumstances.

Additionally, the conflict between the sexes plays a critical role in "Othello." The women in the play, particularly Desdemona and Emilia, struggle against the restrictive societal norms and misogynistic attitudes of the men around them. This conflict is most evident in Emilia's powerful monologue in Act 4, Scene 3, where she challenges the double standards of fidelity in marriage.

Finally, the undercurrent of deceit and manipulation throughout the play creates an overarching conflict between appearance and reality. Iago, who embodies this conflict, masterfully deceives almost every character, leading to tragic consequences. His pretense of honesty is so convincing that he's often referred to as "honest Iago," despite his devious intentions.

Now, let's start and examine each of the conflicts:

1. Othello and Iago: The main conflict in Shakespeare's tragedy, "Othello," arises between Othello, the Moorish general of the Venetian army, and his ensign, Iago. This conflict primarily manifests as a psychological battle, rooted in Iago's resentment towards Othello.

Iago's perceived slight, caused by Othello's decision to promote Cassio as his lieutenant instead of Iago, ignites the flame of his vengeance. Iago states in Act 1, Scene 1, "I know my price, I am worth no worse a place," showing his disdain for being overlooked. Despite his apparent loyalty towards Othello, Iago harbors a deep-seated resentment that fuels his villainous actions throughout the play.

Iago is a master manipulator who exploits Othello's insecurities about his race and outsider status. He sows seeds of doubt in Othello's mind about his wife Desdemona's fidelity, leading Othello down a destructive path of paranoia, jealousy, and ultimately, murder. Iago's insidious insinuations of Desdemona's infidelity with Cassio, although entirely baseless, deeply affect Othello, who comes to believe them without concrete evidence. Iago's infamous monologue in Act 2, Scene 3, "I'll pour this pestilence into his ear," confirms his intent to poison Othello's mind with jealousy.

The complexity of the conflict between Othello and Iago lies in the disparity between appearances and reality. Othello believes in Iago's honesty, referring to him as "honest Iago," which makes him an easy prey for Iago's manipulations. Meanwhile, Iago cleverly conceals his malevolence, continuing to pledge his allegiance to Othello, and even seemingly advising him against jealousy in Act 3, Scene 3, "O, beware, my lord, of jealousy; It is the green-eyed monster which doth mock the meat it feeds on."

This layered conflict drives the narrative and provides an insightful exploration of the human capacity for manipulation, deceit, and the catastrophic consequences of unbridled jealousy. The tragic unraveling of the noble hero Othello, under the influence of Iago's malignant manipulation, underpins the heart-wrenching tragedy of the play.

2. Othello and Desdemona: The conflict between Othello and Desdemona is less a clash of personalities and more a tragic misunderstanding fueled by Iago's machinations. Their relationship starts as a romantic idyll, with Othello winning Desdemona's love through his thrilling stories of adventure, and Desdemona defying societal norms to marry a man of different race and status. However, this love story takes a tragic turn due to the poisonous seeds of jealousy sown by Iago.

Once Iago plants the idea of Desdemona's infidelity into Othello's mind, Othello's trust in Desdemona gradually disintegrates. His love turns into suspicion and then violent jealousy. In Act 3, Scene 3, Othello states, "Why did I marry? This honest creature doubtless sees and knows more, much more, than he unfolds," showing his growing suspicion. Desdemona's pleas of innocence only serve to confirm Othello's unfounded suspicions.

Desdemona, unaware of the cause of Othello's change in demeanor, remains committed to her husband. Her loyalty and innocence become apparent in Act 5, Scene 2, where she pleads with Othello before her death,

"And have you mercy too! I never did offend you in my life." Even in death, Desdemona defends Othello, attributing her death to herself rather than him. Her last words show the extent of her love and loyalty, making her fate all the more tragic.

The conflict between Othello and Desdemona tragically exemplifies the damaging power of jealousy and the ultimate victimization of innocence. This relationship demonstrates how trust, once broken, can lead to devastating consequences.

3. Othello and Cassio: The conflict between Othello and Cassio arises from Iago's manipulation. Cassio, who is initially Othello's trusted lieutenant, finds himself at the receiving end of Othello's wrath due to a series of events orchestrated by Iago.

Cassio loses his position as lieutenant due to his drunken brawl in Act 2, Scene 3. The incident not only creates a rift between Othello and Cassio but also provides Iago with a chance to further his plot. Cassio's demotion and his subsequent attempts to regain his position with the help of Desdemona, unknowingly play into Iago's plan. Iago uses these circumstances to create an illusion of an affair between Desdemona and Cassio, which fuels Othello's jealousy and mistrust.

The irony lies in the fact that both Othello and Cassio are victims of Iago's manipulations, with their conflict being a result of misunderstandings and misconceptions. The tragic nature of their conflict is emphasized in Act 5, Scene 2, where Othello regrets his actions towards Cassio after discovering Iago's deceit.

4. Iago and Emilia: Iago and Emilia's relationship is a stark contrast to that of Othello and Desdemona. It is characterized by manipulation, a lack of trust, and an extreme power imbalance. Iago treats Emilia more as a pawn in his scheme than a wife, using her loyalty to further his plot against Othello.

Emilia is unwittingly involved in Iago's plot when she picks up Desdemona's handkerchief, which becomes the concrete "proof" of Desdemona's alleged infidelity. Emilia's realization of her role in the tragic outcome is evident in Act 5, Scene 2, where she exclaims, "Oh, my God, a guilt so full of lies!" This realization prompts Emilia to reveal Iago's actions, leading to the ultimate unraveling of Iago's plots.

This conflict is more subtle but critical. Iago's treatment of Emilia reflects his views on women and his manipulative nature. Emilia's eventual defiance highlights her moral courage and provides a powerful counterpoint to Iago's deceit.

5. Iago and Roderigo: Roderigo is a wealthy, somewhat foolish man who is infatuated with Desdemona and is led to believe by Iago that he has a chance with her. Their relationship is a clear example of manipulation, as Iago uses Roderigo's love for Desdemona to his advantage, exploiting his wealth and foolhardiness.

Roderigo becomes Iago's puppet, executing his plans under the impression that it will lead him to Desdemona. This is particularly evident in Act 1, Scene 3, where Iago says to Roderigo, "Thus do I ever make my fool my purse," indicating his clear exploitation of Roderigo. Roderigo's eventual realization of Iago's manipulation comes too late, culminating in a deadly confrontation in Act 5.

6. Desdemona and Brabantio: The conflict between Desdemona and her father, Brabantio, stems from her elopement with Othello. Brabantio, a Venetian senator, is shocked and feels betrayed by his daughter's secret marriage to Othello, a man of different race and culture.

In Act 1, Scene 3, Brabantio accuses Othello of using magic to win Desdemona, a reflection of his disbelief that Desdemona could genuinely love Othello. He tells the Duke, "She, in spite of nature, / Of years, of country, credit, everything, / To fall in love with what she feared to look on!" This conflict reveals racial and societal prejudices of the time and underscores the theme of otherness in the play.

Desdemona defends her love for Othello, showing her courage and commitment. Her response to Brabantio and the senators, "I do perceive here a divided duty," signals her defiance of societal norms in favor of her love for Othello. However, the clash with her father sets the stage for the tragic events to follow.

7. Othello and Society: Othello's conflict with society is central to the narrative. As a black man in predominantly white Venice, Othello's outsider status is constantly underlined. His difference is amplified not just by his race but also by his profession as a military leader. His valor makes him a respected figure, but his racial difference remains a point of prejudice.

This societal conflict becomes personal when Othello marries Desdemona. Brabantio's reaction, as mentioned earlier, is a stark reminder of the societal norms Othello defies by his marriage. The racial slurs used by Iago and Roderigo, calling Othello "the thick-lips" (Act 1, Scene 1) or "an old black ram" (Act 1, Scene 1), further underscore this societal conflict.

8. Cassio and Bianca: The relationship between Cassio and Bianca provides a subplot that is manipulated by Iago to serve his larger scheme. Bianca, a courtesan, is in love with Cassio, but he does not reciprocate her deep feelings. The handkerchief that Cassio gives to Bianca, initially a token of love from Othello to Desdemona, becomes a symbol of infidelity and deceit, fueling Othello's jealousy.

In Act 4, Scene 1, Bianca's confrontation with Cassio over the handkerchief, which she believes is a gift from another woman, is misconstrued by Othello as an argument between lovers, furthering his belief in Desdemona's infidelity. This conflict, while minor, is significant in driving the central plot towards its tragic climax.

The intricate relationships and conflicts in "Othello" underline the play's exploration of jealousy, deceit, and the destructive power of manipulation. These conflicts, whether rooted in love, trust, societal norms, or personal ambitions, contribute significantly to the tragic arc of the narrative.

WHAT MAKES THIS PLAY A TRAGEDY

"Othello" is a tragedy due to its exploration of the destructive consequences of jealousy, deceit, and societal prejudices. It follows the classic structure of a tragedy, where a heroic figure is led to downfall through a combination of personal flaws and external influences. The tragic outcome is both an inevitable result of the characters' actions and a cautionary tale about unchecked passions and manipulation.

The tragic hero, Othello, is a respected general who is brought to ruin by a fatal flaw, or 'hamartia'. In Othello's case, it's his propensity for jealousy and his tendency to trust in appearances. His fall from grace is tragic because he starts the play as a noble, respected, and successful man. Yet, under Iago's manipulation, his jealousy spirals out of control until he murders his innocent wife, Desdemona, in a fit of unfounded rage. His tragic end arrives when he, realizing his terrible mistake, takes his own life.

The tragic impact of "Othello" also lies in the demise of innocent characters like Desdemona and Emilia. Desdemona, a young woman who defies societal norms to marry Othello, dies undeservingly at the hands of her husband. Emilia, Iago's wife and Desdemona's loyal maid, also meets a tragic end when she reveals her husband's villainy, even though she had been an unwitting participant in his plot.

Iago's machinations embody the tragic elements of deceit and manipulation. Iago masterfully manipulates the other characters, exploiting their vulnerabilities for his personal vendetta. His unmasking at the end of the play underlines the tragic consequences of his deceptions.

Moreover, the tragedy in "Othello" is amplified by the themes of societal prejudice and racism. Othello is an outsider in Venetian society, and this "otherness" is exploited by Iago and causes Othello to doubt his wife's fidelity. These societal prejudices, combined with Othello's internalized insecurities, significantly contribute to the tragic events of the play.

The play's tragic element is further cemented through its exploration of the destructive power of unchecked passions. Jealousy, referred to as the "green-eyed monster" in Act 3, Scene 3, becomes an uncontrollable force that leads to multiple deaths.

Lastly, the sense of inevitable doom hanging over the characters adds to the play's tragic essence. The audience, aware of Iago's plot, experiences dramatic irony, forced to watch helplessly as the characters march towards their tragic ends.

In conclusion, "Othello" is a tragedy due to its tale of the downfall of a noble hero, the demise of innocent characters, the destructive power of jealousy and deceit, and the exploration of societal prejudices. The play serves as a grim reminder of the disastrous outcomes that can result from unchecked emotions, deceit, and societal biases, offering a profound critique of these human and societal flaws.

—·—

CLIMAX OF THE PLAY

The climax of "Othello," by William Shakespeare, is a moment of profound dramatic tension and tragic revelation. This point comes in Act 5, Scene 2, when Othello murders Desdemona, the truth about Iago's manipulation is revealed, and Othello takes his own life in remorse.

The scene opens with Othello standing over the sleeping Desdemona, preparing to kill her as a punishment for the adultery he believes she has committed with Cassio. Despite his resolution, Othello's love for Desdemona is evident, as he states he "will not kill thy unprepared spirit," and he kisses her one last time before he takes her life. Desdemona awakens and pleas for her life, maintaining her innocence till the very end, but Othello is consumed by misguided jealousy and smothers her.

Emilia's entrance soon after Desdemona's death marks the beginning of the revelation and the tragic aftermath. When Emilia discovers that Desdemona is dead and hears Othello's reason for killing her, she vehemently denies the accusations against Desdemona. Despite Othello's attempts to explain Iago's involvement, Emilia refuses to believe her husband could be responsible. Still, driven by loyalty towards Desdemona and outrage at her unjust death, she exposes Iago's manipulation, shouting for help and declaring, "My husband says she was false!"

Iago, followed by Montano and Graziano, arrive at the scene. When Emilia repeats Othello's claims and insists that Iago has lied, Iago threatens her, but she continues to reveal his deceit, saying, "Thou art rash as fire, to say / That she was false." At this point, Othello realizes he has been manipulated, and the full extent of Iago's treachery is revealed. Othello attacks Iago, but is disarmed by Montano.

As the truth unravels, the depth of Iago's manipulation becomes evident. When Iago kills Emilia for revealing his plot, the sense of tragedy escalates. Despite being mortally wounded, Emilia does not recant her words, dying beside her mistress.

The tragic climax concludes with Othello's intense remorse and self-loathing, as he grapples with the realization that his jealousy and Iago's lies led him to murder his innocent wife. He kisses Desdemona's lifeless body and, using a hidden weapon, stabs himself. His last words, "I kissed thee ere I killed thee: no way but this, / Killing myself, to die upon a kiss," encapsulate the tragic mix of love and despair that drove his actions.

In conclusion, the climax of "Othello" is a potent mix of death, deceit, revelation, and remorse. It's a tragic culmination of Iago's manipulations and Othello's fatal flaws, serving as a profound exploration of the destructive power of jealousy and the devastating consequences of deceit. This climax, marked by the deaths of Desdemona, Emilia, and Othello, is a chilling reminder of the pernicious effects of uncontrolled emotions and unchecked manipulations.

— • —

RESOLUTION OF THE PLAY

The resolution of "Othello" takes place in Act 5, Scene 2, after the tragic climax where Othello kills Desdemona and then himself, following the revelation of Iago's treacherous manipulations.

Here's how it unfolds:

Emilia, Iago's wife, arrives to find the tragic scene of Desdemona's lifeless body. Upon hearing Othello's reasoning for murdering Desdemona, she immediately recognizes the handkerchief, the critical 'evidence' of Desdemona's supposed infidelity, as the one she had innocently given to Iago. Realizing her husband's malevolent scheme, she reveals it to those present.

Iago, who has arrived in the meantime, tries to silence Emilia but fails. She cries out, exposing his deceit to the remaining characters, which include Montano, Gratiano, and Lodovico. Overcome by his failure to control the situation, Iago stabs Emilia, who continues to decry his villainy until she dies.

With Iago's manipulations laid bare, Othello is devastated by the realization of Desdemona's innocence and his own folly. In a fit of overwhelming guilt, he stabs himself and dies next to Desdemona, making a final proclamation of his love for her.

Iago refuses to speak or justify his actions when he's arrested, leaving the characters and the audience to grapple with his senseless malice. Lodovico, a nobleman from Venice, takes charge, delegating the punishment of Iago to Cassio and setting the stage for a return to order after the tragic events. He and the remaining characters are left to mourn and reflect on the tragic sequence of events, and Lodovico prepares to return to Venice, taking with him the grievous news of Othello and Desdemona's deaths.

So, the resolution brings a sense of closure, yet it is permeated with a deep tragedy. The villain is unmasked and justice is promised, but it comes too late for Othello and Desdemona. The play concludes with a sober reflection on the destructive power of jealousy, manipulation, and mistrust, leaving the audience with a poignant sense of regret and the inefficacy of justice after such immense loss.

Moral of this play

The play "Othello" by William Shakespeare, one of his most powerful and intense tragedies, presents us with several complex themes and morals that resonate with audiences even centuries after it was written. These can be summarized as follows:

1. **Destructive Power of Jealousy**: One of the most critical morals in "Othello" is the destructive power of jealousy, aptly represented by Othello's transformation from a rational, loving husband into a murderous agent of revenge. As Iago plants seeds of doubt in Othello's mind about Desdemona's fidelity, we witness the disastrous effects of unchecked jealousy. Othello's jealousy overpowers his reason, leading him to trust Iago's insinuations over Desdemona's protestations of innocence. This "green-eyed monster" makes him blind to reality, ultimately causing the deaths of both Desdemona and himself. The play, therefore, serves as a stark warning of how jealousy can distort our perception and lead to ruin.

2. **Manipulation and Deceit**: Iago's manipulative nature and deceitful actions remind us of the harm that dishonesty can cause. He masterfully manipulates people's weaknesses, using their trusts and fears against them, to weave a web of lies that leads to tragedy. Iago's deception not only underlines the importance of honesty in human relationships but also warns of the dangers

posed by individuals who exploit trust for their nefarious ends.

3. **Prejudices and Stereotyping**: "Othello" exposes the damaging effects of prejudices and stereotypes. Despite being a respected military commander, Othello, as a Moor, is an outsider in Venetian society and subjected to racial prejudice. His perceived 'otherness' makes him vulnerable to Iago's manipulations, who plays on his insecurities related to his racial identity. This aspect of the play underlines the importance of judging people by their character rather than their racial or ethnic backgrounds.

4. **Tragic Consequences of Trusting the Wrong People**: Othello's downfall is precipitated by his misplaced trust in Iago. Meanwhile, Desdemona's loyalty to her husband, even when he accuses her unjustly, tragically leads to her death. The play suggests the necessity of discernment in placing trust and the dire consequences of misplaced trust.

5. **Female Subjugation and Misogyny**: The female characters in "Othello" endure mistreatment, from Desdemona's undeserved murder to Emilia's exploitation by Iago. The tragic outcomes they face underscore the effects of misogyny and the objectification of women. The women in "Othello," despite their strength and integrity, are powerless in a society dominated by men, highlighting the need for gender equality.

6. **Importance of Self-Knowledge and Confidence**: Othello's insecurity about his outsider status in Venetian society makes him susceptible to Iago's manipulations. His lack of self-confidence and self-knowledge allows Iago to sow the seeds of doubt and jealousy. This theme suggests the importance of self-knowledge and confidence in resisting external manipulations.

7. **Futility of Revenge**: The play ultimately shows the futility of revenge. Iago's complex scheme of revenge leads not to satisfaction but to the loss of his wife and his freedom, along with the deaths of Othello, Desdemona, and Roderigo. This underlines the moral that revenge does not lead to resolution but instead perpetuates a cycle of violence and tragedy.

In essence, "Othello" is a cautionary tale about the dangers of jealousy, the pernicious effects of manipulation and deceit, the destructive power of prejudice, and the importance of trust, honesty, and self-knowledge. The morals drawn from the play serve as timeless reminders of these fundamental aspects of human nature and society.

— • —

FAMOUS LINES FROM THE PLAY

"Othello" is rich in memorable lines that reflect the depth of its characters and the thematic intensity of the play. Here are some of the most famous quotes:

1. **"O, beware, my lord, of jealousy; It is the green-ey'd monster, which doth mock The meat it feeds on."** (Act 3, Scene 3)
   This is Iago's warning to Othello, a masterful bit of manipulation wherein he instills the very jealousy he warns against.

2. **"I am not what I am."** (Act 1, Scene 1)
   This is one of Iago's most chilling lines, revealing his duplicitous nature.

3. **"I kissed thee ere I killed thee: no way but this; Killing myself, to die upon a kiss."** (Act 5, Scene 2)
   Othello speaks these heartbreaking lines after he's killed Desdemona, and just before he kills himself.

4. **"She loved me for the dangers I had pass'd, And I loved her that she did pity them."** (Act 1, Scene 3)
   Othello says this to the Duke, explaining how his tales of adventure led to his romance with Desdemona.

5. **"Tis neither here nor there."** (Act 4, Scene 3)
   Emilia speaks this line, meaning that something is of little conse-

quence. This phrase is still widely used today.

6. **"Reputation, reputation, reputation! O, I have lost my reputation! I have lost the immortal part of myself, and what remains is bestial."** (Act 2, Scene 3)
Cassio laments the loss of his reputation after he is dismissed from his position due to drunken behavior.

7. **"It is the cause, it is the cause, my soul."** (Act 5, Scene 2)
Othello mutters this to himself before he kills Desdemona, trying to convince himself that he is justified in killing her because of her supposed infidelity.

8. **"Heaven is my judge, not I for love and duty, But seeming so, for my peculiar end."** (Act 1, Scene 1)
In this line, Iago expresses his cynical and manipulative view of service and duty.

9. **"I will wear my heart upon my sleeve For daws to peck at; I am not what I am."** (Act 1, Scene 1)
Again, Iago's words reveal his manipulative and deceitful nature, making it clear that he hides his true intentions.

10. **"But I do love thee! and when I love thee not, Chaos is come again."** (Act 3, Scene 3)
Othello tells Desdemona he loves her and that his world would be in chaos if he did not. Tragically, it is his love that turns into destructive jealousy.

These lines are significant as they often encapsulate the broader themes of the play - jealousy, love, deceit, and tragedy. They also offer profound insights into the complex characters that inhabit Shakespeare's tragic world in "Othello."